CW01661119

The Wizard Within

The Wizard Within

The Krasner Method of Hypnotherapy

by

Dr. A.M. Krasner

Santa Ana, CA
2001

Third Edition

Published by American Board of Hypnotherapy Press
2002 E. McFadden, Suite 100, Santa Ana, CA 92705

ISBN 1-931116-03-2

Artwork & cover by Crafty Graphics, Santa Ana, CA

Designed and produced with the assistance of
Christopher Burkhardt, Santa Ana, CA

Printed in the United States of America

to Arlene

ACKNOWLEDGEMENTS

I am deeply grateful to many people for making this book possible.

I want to thank the entertainer who gave me the idea.

I want to thank my dedicated and tireless staff who spent so many hours in proofreading and editing the material. In particular, I would like to acknowledge the hard work and assistance of Caroline Miller, Ph.D. Dr. Miller's help was invaluable in the preparation of this text.

Dr. Masud Ansari prepared the index for this Second Edition, a well-done and greatly appreciated task.

Christopher Burkhardt handled the design, and the artists at Crafty Graphics did a beautiful job on all the artwork...thank you.

Most of all, though, I want to thank my students and patients who, over the years, have taught me everything I know...and are teaching me still.

TABLE OF CONTENTS

FOREWORD

Hypnosis, the oldest and most natural mode of healing known to man, is considered to be a potent and safe adjunct to medicine as well as an effective procedure in psychotherapy. For thousands of years, philosophers and intellectuals have known that thoughts can control the body's functions and human behavior—that within us all there is the potential to uplift, heal and inspire others as well as ourselves. That this potential flows throughout all mankind gives us the assurance that there is no such thing as a totally helpless situation or an insurmountable problem. Hypnosis is considered to be the best tool to access, mobilize and actualize this potential.

Unfortunately, this wonderful modality of hypnosis remains somewhat cloaked in the veil of mysticism. Dr. A.M. Krasner, an established and highly qualified authority on the subject, strips hypnosis of its occult rainment by presenting it as a powerful therapeutic tool.

Dr. Krasner drew on his years of research, teaching and clinical experience to establish the American Institute of Hypnotherapy, the first educational institution to offer postgraduate degree programs in hypnotherapy. He is making great strides toward establishing the fields of hypnosis and hypnotherapy as independent faculties of science, much as Freud did with psychology at the turn of the century.

Through scientific research, clinical application and teaching experiences, Dr. Krasner has turned the "magic" of hypnosis into specific, understandable procedures that demonstrate it to be the worthy, serious field of behavioral science that it is.

"The Wizard Within" describes the phenomena of hypnosis, with applicable techniques, and clearly details the history of related areas of hypnotherapy during the last 20 years, including neuro-linguistic programming

(NLP) and dual brain hemisphere functions. Dr. Krasner successfully takes therapeutic hypnosis from its formative stages to normative usage. By delving into the roots of human conditioning and habit formation, the book analyzes the psychobiology of human behavior and effective methods to eradicate negative and harmful habits.

This superb collection of theories and techniques will be a source of inspiration for readers who are interested in exploring the unfathomed world of hypnosis, including self-hypnosis, as well as for practitioners who want to enhance their insight and experiences in clinical hypnosis and hypnotherapy.

Masud Ansari

Masud Ansari, Ph.D., is a prominent psychologist and hypnotherapist with a private practice in Washington, D.C. He is the author of 15 books on political science and law, as well as hypnosis. His ***Modern Hypnosis: Theory and Practice****, is widely considered to be a classic text on the subject. Dr. Ansari earned his doctorate at the George Washington University, and is the past president of the Lebanese Society for Clinical Hypnosis.*

PREFACE

When I was a boy I was, like most other children, enchanted by the story of The Wizard of Oz. Visiting the Land of Oz was a fantasy wish . . . I spent countless hours daydreaming of tripping down the famous Yellow Brick Road to the Emerald City of Oz where dreams came true.

We are all familiar with the story of Dorothy and her dog Toto. They made the perilous journey along the Yellow Brick Road with their companions the Cowardly Lion, the Tin Woodsman and the Scarecrow. The unlikely group went through many exciting adventures and frightening experiences in order to reach the Land of Oz where the Wizard lived. They believed that he—and only he—could grant their wishes.

The Scarecrow wanted brains. The Tin Woodsman wanted a heart. The Lion wanted courage.

Of course, the three of them already had those things; they just didn't believe they did.

After stuffing the Scarecrow's head with a mixture of needles, pins and bran the Wizard of Oz declared, "I have given you brains. Hereafter you will be a great man." The Scarecrow believed the Wizard, and he felt very wise indeed.

The Wizard took a silk heart filled with sawdust and placed it in the Tin Woodsman's breast. The Wizard said, "Now, you have a heart any man would be proud of." The Tin Woodsman believed the Wizard, and he felt tender and loving.

The Lion drank a special potion which, according to the Wizard, was courage. "Drink this," said the Wizard, "and you will be filled with courage." The Lion, believing the Wizard, drank the potion, and he feared nothing.

Never mind that the Wizard of Oz turned out to be an ordinary man; he was extraordinary in that he had the capacity to engender belief, to change the course of people's lives by changing their beliefs about themselves.

During the course of the story, the three had many occasions to demonstrate their newly discovered brains, heart and courage as they faced the dangerous task of getting Dorothy and Toto back to Kansas.

They all performed perfectly. The Scarecrow was brilliant, the Tin Woodsman was kind and helpful and the Lion was fearlessly courageous. They knew they could do these things ... The Wizard of Oz had told them so, and they believed him.

Naturally as I grew older, I didn't dwell on the story any longer. My fantasy trips to the Land of Oz were precluded by "grown-up" matters, such as raising a family and developing my profession.

For the past twenty years, I have been a hypnotherapist. Teaching hypnosis has been my focus for the past decade. I am constantly searching for ways to do it better.

I hadn't thought of the Wizard of Oz in years, in fact, until recently when I was listening to an entertainer recount the familiar tale. I was suddenly struck with the obvious metaphor that it presents. How better, I thought, to help people understand the unconscious mind and its power than to compare it to the wonderful Wizard of Oz?

Everyone knows that the Wizard is powerful and capable of making dreams come true. But did you know that you have your own resident Wizard, constantly and unerringly carrying out your commands? Whatever is happening in your life right now is undoubtedly a result of the orders your Wizard receives and carries out.

Is there something about yourself that you want to change or improve? I am absolutely convinced that you can make that change or improvement with hypnosis. Twenty years of experience and thousands of clients have proved it to me.

Through hypnosis you can change your beliefs and the "orders" you have been giving your magical Wizard

Within. Hypnosis is your Yellow Brick Road. I invite you to travel it to a happier, healthier, more productive life.

—AMK

CHAPTER ONE

WHAT IS HYPNOSIS?

What is hypnosis? Ask two hundred experts. I guarantee that you'll get at least two hundred different answers... all of them correct, yet full of contradictions, "I don't knows," and ambiguities. That hypnosis exists is a point of consensus, as is the fact that something happens as a result of it. The definitions depart from there.

The definitions that follow here are from varied sources, all authorities in the field. Some are researchers, some are writers and some are clinicians. You will see that the range of thinking on this single subject is varied and vast as you consider the following:

"Hypnosis is largely a question of your willingness to be receptive and responsive to ideas, and to allow these ideas to act upon you without interference. These ideas we call suggestions." (Weitzenhoffer and Hilgard)

"Hypnosis is a state of intensified attention and receptiveness to an idea or to a set of ideas." (Erickson)

"Hypnosis is a particular altered state of selective hypersuggestibility brought about in an individual by the use of a combination of relaxation, fixation of attention and suggestion." (Ansari)

"Hypnosis is a state of relatively heightened susceptibility to prestige suggestions." (Hull)

"Hypnosis is an altered state of the organism originally and usually produced by a repetition of stimuli in which suggestion (no matter how defined) is more effective than usual." (Marcuse)

"Hypnosis is an altered state within which suggestions have a peculiarly potent effect." (Bowers)

"Hypnosis is nothing but an aspect of conditioning." (Salter)

"In hypnosis the subconscious, having no power to reason, accepts and acts upon any fact or suggestion given to it by the conscious mind." (Caprio and Berger)

Enough, you say? The list is virtually endless! However, in addition to showing any array of opinions, the above quotations contain common threads, some of which are almost always present in anyone's definition: altered state, conscious/subconscious functioning and heightened suggestibility.

Common sense tells us that if we are to communicate effectively with each other, we must reach an agreement on our understanding of the meanings of words. I have been in this profession far too long not to have developed my own definition of hypnosis. I offer it here not to disagree with the eminent professionals I quoted, but to clarify my own position for this book.

I believe hypnosis to be *a process which produces relaxation, distraction of the conscious mind, heightened suggestibility and increased awareness, allowing access to the subconscious mind through the imagination. It also produces the ability to experience thoughts and images as real.*

For the process to be effective, there are two components that must be present: Belief and Expectation. In my classes, I teach the simple formula, *BELIEF* + *EXPECTATION* = *HYPNOSIS.*

BELIEF—OUR GUIDING PRINCIPLES

When we think of the word *"belief,"* we often think in terms of creeds of doctrines. *"I believe in America." "I believe that criminals should be punished." "I believe what my leader says."* Those statements are indeed statements of belief. However, at the most basic level, in the deepest sense, a belief is a guiding principle that gives direction and meaning to life. Our beliefs form the basis for our perceptions of the world.

When we believe something or believe in something, we are delivering a message to the brain about what is occurring. The brain then orders the body how to respond. Beliefs have great powers in our lives. You will encounter much more on this in later chapters.

EXPECTATION—
THE SELF-FULFILLING PROPHECY

The American sociologist W.I. Thomas was the first to set forth the theorem: "If men define situations as real, they are real in their consequences." R. K. Merton, professor of sociology at Columbia University, elaborated on this concept—the Self-Fulfilling Prophecy—by stating that when we predict an event, the expectation of the event changes our behavior in such a way to make the event more likely to happen.

We have all seen examples of this phenomenon:

- The lion tamer who loses his nerve is the most vulnerable to attack.
- The student with "exam anxiety," convinced that he will fail, spends more time worrying than studying, and he does poorly on the exam.

According to Merton, the Self-Fulfilling Prophecy is, in the beginning, a false definition or belief, about a situation. This false belief causes a new behavior that makes the false belief come true. The circle of error is then perpetuated, for the "prophet" will cite the actual course of events as proof that he was right from the very beginning.

Why does the Self-Fulfilling Prophecy exist? We are reassured by predictive accuracy; we do not like to be surprised. We want others to be as we expect them to be—it makes us feel secure.

Therefore, if a person has the belief that he can be hypnotized and the expectation that he will be hypnotized, then he will be hypnotized—every time.

MYTHS, MISCONCEPTIONS AND FEARS ABOUT HYPNOSIS

The great researcher Clark Hull said, "All sciences alike have descended from magic and superstition, but none has been so slow as hypnosis in shaking off the evil association of its origin."

No doubt you are familiar with the stereotypical image of the mysterious, robe-and-turban-clad man swinging a pocket watch in front of a helpless, not-too-intelligent, near-catatonic subject, saying, "You are in my power."

I'm sure most people agree that such an image is ridiculous. However, the fact remains that there are many existing misconceptions that result in real fears concerning hypnosis, and I believe that most of them originated with the above image.

MYTH OF THE WEAK MIND

Incredibly, there exists a pervasive belief that only the weak-minded and/or gullible can be hypnotized. Actually, quite the opposite is true. People of above average intelligence who are capable of concentrating and those who have active, vivid imaginations . . . make the best hypnotic subjects.

FEAR OF REVEALING SECRETS

I still regularly encounter people who have genuine concerns that if they allow themselves to be hypnotized, they will "tell all", and reveal some secret from their past that they wish to keep. The illusion that hypnosis is a "power relationship" between the hypnotherapist and the subject runs very deep in public consciousness. Many still think that if they are hypnotized that they have no choice but to obey the commands given them. Yet, in truth, the hypnotherapist-subject relationship is anything but a power relationship. The only "power" lies in the mind of the subject because in hypnosis, he has greater awareness than when he is fully awake, and he completely retains his powers of selectivity. His secrets are secure.

FEAR OF HUMILIATION

Who wants to be made to look like a fool? Nobody, certainly. However, it is not unusual to find that a person's entire knowledge of hypnosis is based on what he saw in a stage show! Unfortunately, the "Svengali Syndrome" has been fostered through the media by modern stage hypnotists. It is necessary for the audience to have an element of this false belief for the show to be entirely successful. Therefore, I say to the skeptical, fearful client: "The people who are the stage subjects volunteered to participate, didn't they? They knew that in doing so, they would be acting silly, clowning around and just generally being funny, didn't they?" The answer is always yes, of course. The people who volunteer for shows do so with complete knowledge of what is to come. They are generally uninhibited, fun-loving people who realize that a hypnosis show is meant to be enjoyment for everyone involved. Volunteer subjects expect to participate in an entertaining show, and they know that the audience, likewise, expects to be entertained.

To repeat what I said earlier, *the power of selectivity prevails in the hypnotic state.* Therefore, a subject may never be induced into hurting himself or "fooled" into committing a crime. However, if for any reason the subject finds a suggestion objectionable, he will either refuse to participate, or he will spontaneously and completely come out of hypnosis.

Therefore, if a stage subject is asked to imitate a clown or quack like a duck, he will cheerfully comply. But what if he is asked to rob a bank? Never. He would come out of hypnosis and end the show.

FEAR OF LOSS OF CONTROL

"I don't want anyone to control my mind!"

This is a classic fear that, like the others, stems from past negative and false images. A hypnotized subject is in full control of himself, fully aware of the environment and completely capable of making decisions. If the subject is presented with an idea or suggestion that he finds objectionable in full consciousness, rest assured that he will find it equally objectionable in hypnosis, and he will reject it outright. As explained in the above section, it may even cause him to come out of hypnosis altogether. Hypnosis, then, cannot MAKE him do anything. It only helps him to accomplish the goals he sets for himself.

To demonstrate this in my classes, I put a student volunteer into light hypnosis. I ask him to put his hands by his side, to close his eyes and to let his head fall forward on his chest.

I then say, "Now go into the corner, please, and stand on your head."

Of course, the student does not comply. Instead, his eyes open, his head comes up, he grins and says, "No way!"

I repeat once more: a hypnotized person will simply not accept an objectionable suggestion. In the unlikely event that an emergency such as a fire presented itself, the subject, again, would come out of hypnosis on his own, immediately and fully. The subject is always the one in control.

FEAR OF "THE TRANCE"

I personally do not like to use the word "trance." It seems to evoke images of our earlier-described watch-swinging friend and further promotes a false expectation that hypnosis will produce a "weird feeling."

The term "trance" came from a Middle-English and Old French words *transe*, which meant great anxiety and fear, and *transir*, to perish, and the Latin *transire*, to die. It is easy to see where the morbid, negative connotations originated. The term referred to death itself or to the morbid anxiety and paralyzing fear which preceded death. No wonder the *transe* came to be feared! (Some believe that the Latin term meant "transition", but this is a modern way of thinking about death. For thousands of years, death came by wounds from accidents or battle, or from uncontrolled disease. Few of our ancestors died peacefully; death was always horribly grim and frequently agonizing. Thus the word "trance" originally had death-like qualities.)

Contemporary use of the word "trance" falls into several categories which have become rather well-defined through common usage. When the word is used today, most people think of it in the following contexts:

1. A state resembling sleep, in which consciousness may

remain although voluntary movement is lost.
2. A stunned condition; daze, stupor.
3. A condition of great mental abstraction, especially one induced by religious fervor or mysticism; in recent years, a state induced by chemical means, such as psychedelic drugs.
4. A condition in which a spiritualist medium allegedly loses consciousness and passes under the control of some external force, as for the supposed transmission of a communication from the dead.

You can see what a poor word "trance" is to describe the hypnotic state. I prefer to stay entirely away from it just to avoid the negative suggestions it may carry.

"I WASN'T HYPNOTIZED. I HEARD EVERY WORD YOU SAID."

One of the biggest barriers many people have in experiencing hypnosis is their expectation (and sometimes insistence) that it be a state of unconsciousness or sleep! They cannot quite seem to grasp the simple idea that if hypnosis equalled sleep or unconsciousness, then there would be no such thing as hypnosis or hypnotists! To the person who says, "I don't think I was hypnotized—I heard every word you said," I often answer, "When you wake up each morning, do you feel you've been hypnotized? If not, why not? After all, if you insist that you must be literally asleep or "blacked out" and unconscious in order to feel hypnotized, then why don't you feel hypnotized on those occasions when you actually have been asleep or unconscious?"

As I explained before, there simply is no mysterious "feeling" to being hypnotized. The subject hears everything that is said. He is completely, even acutely aware of everything going on around him. His attention is much more focused in hypnosis than in the normal waking state. The only special "feeling" of being hypnotized is the feeling of total and complete relaxation ... something to look forward to, but never to fear!

FEAR OF NOT "WAKING UP"

There are superficial similarities between hypnosis and sleep, but the fact is that HYPNOSIS IS NOT SLEEP. The two states (sleep and hypnosis) are different both psychologically and physiologically. Although I regularly use the terms "wake up" and "awakening", "waking up" is technically inappropriate terminology. A person just does not "get stuck" in a hypnotic state. It can't happen. What might happen, though, is that he may enjoy the relaxed state so much that he does not want to come back to full waking consciousness just yet. If, for some reason the subject chooses not to come out of hypnosis when instructed to do so, he will, in every case, do one of two things: 1) he will come out on his own in a very short time, or 2) he will fall into a natural sleep until he wakes up naturally.

CHAPTER TWO

THE HISTORY OF HYPNOSIS

Over the years I have reviewed hundreds of books on hypnosis. Most texts contain lengthy chapters on the history of hypnosis, and, I must confess, I sometimes skim (all right, skip) those pages because a litany of names and dates can be quite boring. After all, most of those facts and figures are there only as obligatory introductory material, and, unfortunately, the reader is apt to say, "Who cares?"

However, names and dates notwithstanding, I have come to realize that to understand the history of hypnosis is to understand the history of suggestion; the development of hypnosis through the centuries is directly reflective of man's consciousness in each era.

I find the facts supporting this premise fascinating and worthwhile, and I think you will, too. Suggestion has motivated man since the beginning of time. The "sleep temples" of the ancient Egyptians are depicted in stone dated as early as 1000 B.C. These "temples" were places where priests put worshippers to "sleep" and suggested that they be cured—and they usually were. (These priests actually set forth the procedure for formal hypnotic induction much as it is known and used today.) The success of the Egyptian temples led to their introduction in Greece by the fourth century B.C., and in Rome a hundred years after that. The temples remained popular and functional during the flourishing period of the Roman Empire.

We know that witch doctors, shamans and medicine men have been present in all cultures throughout history. Therefore, the exact timing of the introduction of the "suggestion-sleep and cure" concept throughout Europe is difficult to pinpoint. We do know that it did appear, however, and that it persisted ... and changed, always changing to reflect the culture of the time.

Early in the first century, the practice of "laying on of hands" was introduced. Its therapeutic value was reinforced by the approval of and use by the English monarchy, particularly Edward the Confessor (1042-1066 A.D.), who is famous for practicing and perfecting his "royal touch." So popular was this cure that the procedure was soon recognized by the Church of England to the extent that "proper procedures", complete with appropriate "healing" hymns and chants to facilitate the cures were written into the liturgy. Public acceptance was virtually assured ... After all, the Church was never wrong!

It follows, then, that as royalty eventually lost interest, so did the people. The concept of "suggestion-healing" fell into disrepute and under the cloak of black magic as sorcerers and magicians became its almost sole practitioners in the "civilized" world. The Middle Ages found people distrusting, even fearing those who practiced those methods. It actually came to be considered more evil than beneficial. This period was the time during which many misconceptions were formed which unfortunately still exist.

When the famous Franz Anton Mesmer first appeared on the scene in France (the Mesmer "period" was approximately 1760-1842), public consciousness was not benevolent. Mesmer was tenacious and strong-willed, though, and his "Mesmerism" (or "animal magnetism," as it was also called) soon became popular with the French nobility. As a result, his practice quickly grew to such a proportion that it was impossible to handle. Of course, it is obvious now that "Mesmerism" was nothing more then suggestion . . . but it worked! At one time, reputable sources report that up to three thousand people a day were clamoring for his touch. Here again, we have an example of the power of royalty in the shaping of public consciousness and opinion to the core.

A group of envious physicians and their politician friends formed a commission to investigate and discredit Mesmer. (I found it a particular point of interest to note that Benjamin Franklin was a part of that commission) Mesmer's outrageous behavior and flamboyant personality enraged this austere group, and their zealous efforts against him resulted in his disgraceful exile. Although Mesmer himself was censured, his theories lived on to form the cornerstone for the group psychotherapy and imagery conditioning currently and widely used in therapy today. However, because of the notorious image he created, his contributions are historically perceived as being tinged with black magic.

The first serious physician to study Mesmer's work was Englishman James Braid (1795-1860). He became interested in Mesmerism while watching a demonstration that was part of a carnival show. Convinced that it was a fraud and a swindle, he was determined to make Mesmerism a serious study for the sole purpose of discrediting it once and for all. Instead, he became thoroughly fascinated. His experiments with friends led him to conclude that eye fatigue was necessary to induce the state. He also discovered that a person's susceptibility was increased by a heightened air of expectation. Dr. Braid introduced the term "hypnosis" for the first time, as well as the terms "hypnotist" and "suggestion." The word hypnosis was derived from the Greek *hypnos* which means sleep. By the time Braid came to realize that the word "hypnosis" was misleading and technically incorrect, it had already gained great popularity, and it "stuck," even to this day. In fact, we still use the terms "awaken" and "wake up" when bringing a subject out of hypnosis.

Dr. Braid's method of hypnosis involved virtually no requirement of the hypnotist. He was the first to discover eye-fixation; the subject had only to stare at an object until his eyes tired, and he slipped quite naturally into a hypnotic state. Braid discovered that he could accelerate the process by telling the person, "You are getting very, very sleepy." Braid's work is important to mention here for two reasons: 1) He is responsible for the first permanent shift—however slight—in hypnosis from being considered part of the occult to being regarded as a serious discipline, and 2) even more important, he proved that the true power of hypnosis lies within the individual, that the hypnotist is only of secondary importance.

Dr. James Esdaile (1818-1859), a personal friend and professional colleague of Braid's, began to experiment with hypnotic anesthesia while serving the British East India Company in Calcutta, India. His outstanding success resulted in the lowering of the surgical mortality rate to less than five per cent! He had several years of service in India during which he perfected his techniques and maintained his phenomenal success. Therefore, when he returned to England, he naturally anticipated that his well-established methods would work as well in his homeland as they had worked in India.

They didn't. Why would that be? Think about it. The Indian culture was full of the concepts of "higher self," meditation and other altered states of consciousness, much as it is today. Indian people were conditioned and ready to allow hypnosis to help them. In England, almost the opposite was true. The Church taught that suffering was a noble part of the human condition, that enduring pain established integrity. Consequently, when Esdaile presented his findings in a paper to the British Medical Society, he was laughed to scorn. The Society maintained that Esdaile was interfering with nature.

God created pain; therefore, it was essential for the purification of the soul and the building of character. Esdaile lived out his life in his homeland, a humiliated and broken man.

Chemical anesthesia was discovered in the mid-1800's. You will not be surprised to know that at that point, the physicians changed their attitudes about pain. Suddenly, it was no longer noble to suffer unnecessarily! Queen Victoria's successful chloroform-anesthetized childbirth put the royal seal of approval on the new chemical. The Church became mute on the glories of pain. Physicians began using chloroform and ether with lax abandon. Everyone wanted it! Nurses, orderlies and even clerks administered the pre-surgical magic potion, pouring it on a cloth and putting it on the patient's face. As the operation progressed, more chemical was added. There was no knowledge of the human body's tolerance for these new substances. Now, patients were dying from the anesthesia!

However, chemical anesthetics remained popular and pushed Esdaile's work even further into oblivion at a time when it was badly needed in medicine. Alas, it was back to sideshows and seances for hypnosis.

In the late 1800's, Sigmund Freud became interested in hypnosis, but only for a short while. He abandoned it completely in favor of psychoanalysis, although most experts agree that his free association techniques were only hypnosis by another name.

> Hypnotism is the most practical science of the age. It enters in everyday life, and confers advantages that could not be acquired through any other medium. Its practice is no longer a mere pastime for amusement and sensation, as professional men of the highest standing now recognize its power and seek to profit from its benefits; and scientists regard it as a natural power, for ages kept dormant, but currently destined to perform an active part in the welfare and development of future generations.

> To study hypnotism is like unfathoming the hidden mysteries of magic and human miracles and making them matters of absolute knowledge. Its possibilities are almost boundless and are interwoven with every phase of human life ... It does not require years of study to become a hypnotist for this great blessing to mankind is a natural endowment possessed by all who devote to its study the patience and energy always so necessary for the development of natural talents.

The above quote is an excerpt from "An Introduction to Hypnotism" from the book, *PRACTICAL LESSONS IN HYPNOTISM,* written by William W. Cook, M.D., in 1901. It would seem that the status of hypnotism in 1901 as described by Dr. Cook that the following 90 years would be hypnotherapy's "golden years". Nothing could be further from the truth.

In the early 1900's, a French pharmacist named Emile Coué made a great discovery: the power of autosuggestion which he called "waking suggestion". Coué's famous autosuggestion formula was, *"Every day, in every way, I am getting better and better."* In explaining the waking suggestion formula, Coué wrote:

> Therefore every time you have a pain, physical or otherwise, you will go quietly to your room ... sit down and shut your eyes, pass your hand lightly across your forehead if it is mental distress, or upon the part that hurts, if it is pain in any part of the body, and repeat the words: 'It is going, it is going,' so quickly, that it is impossible for a thought of contrary nature to force itself between the words. We thus actually think it is going, and as all ideas that we fix upon the mind become a reality to us, the pain, physical or mental, vanishes. And should the pain return, repeat the process 10, 20, 50, 100, 200, times if necessary, for it is better to pass the entire day saying: 'It is going!' than to suffer pain

and complain about it.

Coué discovered that the actual suggestion given by the hypnotist accomplished nothing—that accomplishment only occurs when the suggestion is accepted by the mind of the subject. Coué had made this great discovery: *ALL HYPNOSIS IS SELF-HYPNOSIS.* Further, he developed the Laws of Suggestion which I will explain later in this book. These laws, set forth in a system developed by Coué's disciple Charles Baudouin, are still sound and valid today. They explain everything that occurs through suggestion. Because of this essential contribution, I am of the opinion that Coué is the most important and least appreciated figure in the development of hypnosis. His findings provide the framework within which we can understand hypnosis and how it works.

Coué enjoyed immense popularity in his homeland. Thousands of people practiced and benefited from autosuggestion. Things changed abruptly, however, when he brought his theories of autosuggestion to the United States. He made the mistake of putting himself in the hands of a promoter whose attempts to exploit this new "wonder cure" simplified it to the point of ridicule. His original "formula" became the subject of jokes and jingles. Once again, public consciousness caused the acceptance of hypnosis to almost disappear completely, and its existence was again largely considered to be only a part of the mystic underworld.

For the next fifty years, hypnosis had a rather slow and colorless development. It was used some in World War I by the Germans for pain control when they ran out of chemical anesthetics and for treatment of shell-shock during and even after the war.

During those years there were also a few tough-minded individuals who persisted in the study of hypnosis, publishing enough research to keep it alive awhile longer. I consider the most notable of these to be Clark Hull, an American psychologist whose excellent book, *HYPNOSIS AND*

SUGGESTIBILITY, published in 1933, encouraged future generations to study hypnosis.

As a result of World War II and the Korean War, hypnosis was again used for pain control and to aid the mentally crippled. By the 1950's, there was an increasing interest in the medical uses of hypnosis, and in 1958, the American Medical Association approved the therapeutic use of the hypnosis modality. That was a watershed decision.

Since that time, the cyclical development changed to a steady forward progression. Since then, hypnosis has gained acceptance and respectability, a trend that continues today. It is no longer considered to be the exclusive purview of esoteric practitioners. If you care to read about hypnosis, you no longer have to search the metaphysical literature.

Instead, take a look around your local book store in the non-fiction section. Review current periodicals such as *READER'S DIGEST* or *TIME* magazine. Self-hypnosis tapes are for sale wherever tapes are sold. As the public grows familiar with hypnosis, it becomes a more common part of our everyday life.

Today, you don't have to look far to find hypnosis, by whatever name. Call it visualization, relaxation therapy, guided imagery, meditation, whatever. Acceptance of hypnosis is here to stay. Ah, the power of suggestion!

CHAPTER THREE

THE POWER OF SUGGESTION

"I can't help losing my temper—everyone in my family is that way!"

"No matter how hard I try, I just can't lose weight."

"Speaking in public terrifies me. I'm too afraid to try."

"I have a poor memory for names."

"I know I won't sleep. I never can before a test."

"I'm just stuck at this golf score."

"Every time I try, I fail."

"Gloomy days make me sad."

"Every time I see her, I get angry."

Do any of these sound familiar? Such statements are typical of the things we say and hear every single day. Unfortunately, such statements seem to become self-fulfilling prophecies. Do you know why? Each one contains a negative suggestion that becomes a part of the memory bank deep inside the subconscious mind, to be yielded up at a later time for the conscious mind to implement into action.

After all, who among us has not been influenced by suggestion? Suggestion, fueled by imagination, plays a far more important role in our lives than most of us know. Suggestion influences us every day and has done so since our birth. Even the earliest moments of life play an important part in the formations of lifelong habitual attitudes and behavior. As soon as we leave our mother's womb, we become the recipient of suggestions that influence us for the rest of our lives.

Accepted suggestions ultimately become the basis for our personal beliefs which, as stated in Chapter One, are the guiding principles in our lives. Often, the emotional memories of childhood, both good and bad, breed habits in all of us, some of which serve us very well. Unfortunately, some do not.

CHANGE THE INPUT, CHANGE THE OUTPUT

The mind has the capacity for change. We can erase past negative influences and establish new beliefs and new behaviors. We do not have to remain forever locked to behavior patterns that were suitable to the infantile needs of childhood, but are hardly appropriate conduct for the fully functioning adult.

Understand that life is made up of the things that happen to us from the outside, called *input,* combined with the way we react to that input, which is called *output.* That inner belief system that we consequently develop is called our *programming.* Through hypnosis, that programming can be changed to alter our output and transform our lives.

THE CRITICAL FACTOR

Babies and small children are super-susceptible to suggestion, simply because they lack the ability to reason and think logically. Additionally, they have limited stored experiential memory data to draw upon. During those early years, a child will accept whatever he is told, and he believes it to be true. From the age of five or six, he develops a critical faculty, that is, the ability to reason. He can then select what he believes to be true based on his own experiences and emotions. Thereafter, for information to reach his subconscious, it has to bypass that critical factor.

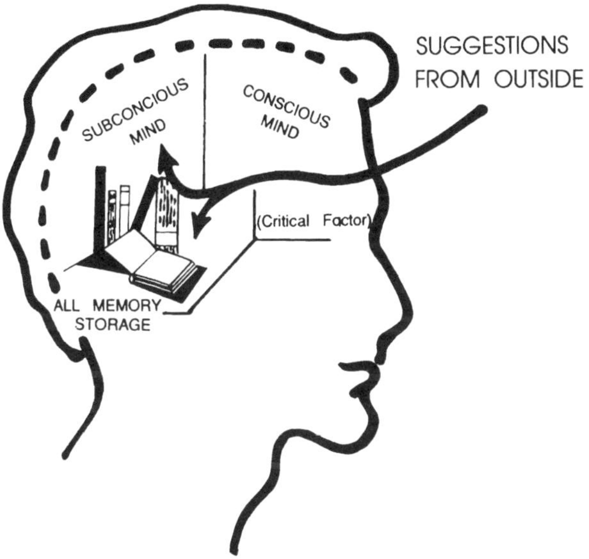

Early outside suggestions bypass the critical factor and enter the subconscious mind.

SUGGESTION PROGRAMMING IN THE EARLY YEARS

According to many child behavioral psychologists, it is during the first six years of life that we develop our strongest personality traits and behavior propensities. We learn to basically trust or distrust other people. We develop a general sense of self-confidence or self-doubt. We establish our sexual identification or gender confusion. We become generally friendly toward other people, or express alienation from them. Additionally, we develop a general initiative to try, or a gloomy fear of failure.

There are a handful of prominent neonatologists (newborn baby physician specialists) who even believe that some of these characteristics are set before the child reaches the age of one. However, whatever the exact age, we know for a fact that our early, formative childhood years provide us with the emotional base upon which we build the rest of our lives.

Even an infant can "sense" a mood change in his parent, and he reacts accordingly. As a child grows, he learns that certain actions, certain words evoke specific responses. For instance, he learns that his mother's smile is his reward for "good" behavior, while her frown or scowl means that she's unhappy, whether or not he caused her feelings. Because it is the nature of a very small child to think that the world revolves around him, he feels responsible for the feelings of the people close to him. Throughout the rest of his life, each word he hears, everything he sees and everything his senses absorb will elicit a particular image and reaction that will be recorded forever in his subconscious mind.

HOW HABITS ARE FORMED

Our physical and emotional reflexes are trained to behave

in a ritualized pattern in accordance with the images we recall. Our brain is constantly flashing information for us to consider. The images it flashes for us include old images, those we stored as children or adolescents, and other images that we pick up from our immediate environment.

Every experience we have leaves its mark on the cortex of the brain. The cortex is the brain's "receiving station" for information fed to it by the nervous system. It is responsible for actually transforming that information into bodily action. Each time an experience is repeated, the mark, or imprint, is strengthened, making it even easier to repeat. Thoughts and behaviors become habitual through repetition.

THE CONDITIONED REFLEX RESPONSE

The type of repetitive behavior described above is called a conditioned reflex response, and it was first discovered and documented by the Russian physiologist Dr. Ivan P. Pavlov. In 1904, Dr. Pavlov received the Nobel Prize for physiology and medicine for his outstanding contribution in tracing patterns of human behavior based on laboratory research with animals.

In his landmark studies with dogs, Pavlov discovered how habits originate and what makes them repetitive.

The test Pavlov used was deceptively simple. He rang a bell, and then he immediately offered food to the dogs. He repeated this many times until he observed that he could ring the bell, and the dogs would salivate whether food was offered to them or not. Amazingly, the dogs would salivate even when they were not hungry. The bell had become a signal to their brains that food was coming, and their brains, in turn, signaled their bodies to start the digestive juices flowing, beginning with the secretion of saliva.

The parallels to be drawn between Pavlov's dogs and human

beings opened up an entirely new scientific view of human behavior. In spite of the fact that human beings had superior intelligence, it was obvious that sensory signals received by the human brain set off identical reflexive behavior as that of the canine.

PEOPLE BEHAVE LIKE TRAINED ANIMALS

We observe and participate in this phenomenon daily. For example, Gerald S. smokes two packs of cigarettes a day. Whenever he drinks coffee, gets in his car, finishes a meal, or performs any number of other "triggering" acts, Gerald lights up. He knows that it is bad for him, but he says that he just "can't help himself." He has "quit" a number of times, but he returns to his habit, each time full of self-loathing, and saying, "I just can't help myself." Each time he quits, he makes the new promise that he will not return to the filthy habit, not ever again. However, his return to cigarettes demonstrates the same theory as Pavlov's dogs did. Gerald associates his cigarette habit with emotional satisfaction, and at the first sign of distress or discomfort, he reaches for a smoke. He also associates cigarettes with physical comfort, so he doesn't feel like he has completed a meal until he's had his cigarette.

Like Pavlov's dogs, we respond to the "bell" in our minds. Simply mention food to a habitual overeater . . . he doesn't even have to be hungry, and he will feel an overwhelming urge to eat. Cigarette smokers, like Gerald above, behave in the same programmed way, responding to signals just like trained animals.

EMOTION—THE MOST IMPORTANT ELEMENT

Dr. Pavlov not only discovered and demonstrated that we become conditioned by repeated suggestions, but he also made another remarkable discovery: suggestions are far more powerful, and acceptance of them is much faster, when the emotions are involved.

Habits are often associated with emotional satisfaction. Any sign of distress causes a reach for the "pacifier," or habit. Pavlov proved that a habit (conditioned reflex) can be established even from just a single input if strong emotion is simultaneously present. Consider the following example which illustrates this fact for both man and animals:

A new mailman approaches a house. The household's pet dog barks at him. The inexperienced mailman reacts foolishly by kicking at the dog. The dog becomes frightened and snaps at the mailman's heels.

The conflict is immediately established. For as long as the mailman and the dog continue to react to each other with fear, the fear perpetuates the reactions, and the reactions become habitual behavior for both the man and the animal. The mailman now reacts with fear when he sees *any* dog, and the dog barks at *every* mailman.

Because of the suggestions we subconsciously accept on a daily basis, we develop a system of beliefs which cause us to react automatically and often without logic. You can easily recognize these automatic reactions, once you are aware they exist. For example, a woman who had a disturbing experience with a man early in life may be heard to repeat, "Isn't that like a man . . . they're all alike!" An almost identical situation occurs for the man who was mistreated early in life by his mother or by some other female. "You just can't trust a woman!" becomes his credo.

We see this principle demonstrated again and again on a more global basis when we observe religious and racial prejudices and attitudes toward specific groups of people. We all know people who automatically distrust redheads (or blondes), dislike all fat people (or thin people), tall people (or short people), etc., etc. Most such conditioned habit reactions have their roots in some emotional experience of the past.

SOME ADDITIONAL CONDITIONED RESPONSES YOU MAY KNOW WELL

Consider the following examples of conditioned response actions that are the result of suggestions received and accepted by the subconscious mind. Remember, these are personalized reflex actions that influence an individual's behavior without his being aware of it, always while he is in a fully awake state:

Music suggests happiness, sadness, dancing, etc ...
Rain suggests freshness, depression, coziness, etc ...
Smells suggest hunger, old memories, nausea, etc ...
Certain people suggest joy, laughter, comfort, etc ...
Certain others suggest tension, sadness, anger, etc ...

Some conditioned responses become so much a part of a person that the responses become habits that affect the individual's everyday life.

Coffee, telephone conversations suggest smoking.
Watching television suggests eating.
A certain place or thing suggests nervousness.

DIFFERENT WAYS IN WHICH WE RECEIVE SUGGESTIONS

Suggestions come to us both verbally and non-verbally. Some of the many ways we both give and receive suggestions every day are as follows:

DIRECTLY

A direct suggestion is any verbal statement or physical action that is to the point, given in a "command" manner.

"Everybody stand up!"
"Eat your food."
"Come here."

INDIRECTLY

Indirect suggestions are primarily non-verbal motions or sounds, and we often respond without being aware of doing so.

Yawn . . . and you cause others to yawn.
Smile . . . and you cause others to smile.
Look upward . . . and you cause others to look upward.

BY INFERENCE

Inferred suggestions are basically the same as indirect suggestions in that they are subtle and often non-verbal. They differ in that they convey a message from one person to another person or group.

Pointing a finger to suggest "Come here" . . .
Nodding your head to indicate affirmation . . .
Making a fist to suggest violent action . . .

FROM PRESTIGE

Prestige suggestions are those we act upon with no questions simply because we respect and believe the authority of the source.

Small children believe their parents.
We believe our physicians.
We believe our teachers.

FROM EMOTIONAL APPEALS

Emotional appeal responses are those that change a person's emotional state, thereby setting into motion any feelings or sensations that the person associates with the event.

Shouting or threats causing panic . . .
Antagonizing or "needling" causing anger . . .
Gentleness or empathy causing happiness or crying.

BY SOCIAL DICTATES

These are suggestions that "lead" or "appeal" to a person's desire to belong, or conform. The phrases "follow the crowd" and "peer pressure" refer to socially-dictated suggestions.

Fashion . . . Hemlines are "up" this year.
Politics . . . That candidate stands for the worker.
Language . . . Words change meaning by increased general usage and acceptance, such as "grass" and "gay".

NEGATIVE CLICHÉ SUGGESTIONS

There are literally hundreds of phrases that are repeated so often that they actually become a part of our belief systems.

You can't make it in this world unless you are rich.
It's not what you know, it's who you know.
You just can't win, no matter how hard you try.

NEGATIVE SUGGESTIONS/
PHYSICAL MANIFESTATIONS

How many times have you heard or said a phrase so often that it becomes true?

He makes me sick.
My job gives me a pain in the neck.
My kids drive me crazy.

POSITIVE SUGGESTIONS

These are the suggestions you are going to learn to formulate and use for yourself to make whatever changes you desire in your life. These are the suggestions that produce self-confidence, inner strength, purpose, calmness, peacefulness.

I am . . .
I can . . .

I'm sure that by now you have thought of many suggestions of your own that fit into the above categories. There are thousands.

As you become aware that you are receiving suggestions almost constantly, you may notice how many negative ones you give yourself . . . several times every day. "I can't, I'm fat, I'm afraid," etc. These suggestions have an immensely powerful influence over how you think, how you feel and how you act, ultimately determining the level of your self-esteem and the quality of your life.

THE GOOD NEWS

So, are people stuck with their habits, helpless victims of circumstances beyond their control? Absolutely not! The power that accepts and stores those negative suggestions, the subconscious mind, is a powerful servo-mechanism, an uncritical, non-judgmental computer. It accepts as true any suggestion that is allowed to bypass that critical factor of the conscious mind to make entrance to its system of memory banks. The body is only a robot acting and performing on command. The computer can be reprogrammed. The old data can be replaced. Through hypnosis, new beliefs and behaviors can be established. Remember:

WE ALWAYS ACT AND FEEL AND PERFORM ACCORDING TO WHAT WE IMAGINE AND BELIEVE TO BE TRUE ABOUT OURSELVES AND OUR SURROUNDINGS.

FIND OUT FOR YOURSELF

To illustrate this, close your eyes, and just think of a lemon. In whatever is your own way, now "see" the lemon's bright yellow color. Feel the waxy surface of the peel and the firmness of the juicy pulp beneath. Now imagine that you are holding the lemon in one hand and a sharp paring knife in the other. When you pierce the lemon with the tip of the knife, you feel a slight spray of liquid that increases as you push the knife down under the peel and into the lemon. Now you can see and feel the juice spurting out and running down your hand. Quickly, you remove the knife, raise the lemon to your mouth and begin to suck the juice.

Now, stop and observe what is happening to you. Are you salivating? Most likely so! But is there a lemon? Only in your imagination! Your mind accepted the suggestion to "see" a lemon, and your body acted accordingly. Remember, the body is only a robot controlled by the brain, completely lacking in the ability to distinguish what is real from what is imagined.

Hypnotherapy takes advantage of the subconscious mind's fundamental creativity: The mind will accept suggestions very quickly if the right connection is made. Acceptable suggestion, linked with the appropriate emotions, is the key.

THE MEDIA AND SUGGESTION

Recently I read an article on information processing that

said we are exposed to over 60,000 bits of information each day! The media certainly knows about suggestion! The average person spends fifteen years of his life in front of the television, and unfortunately, puts a lot of faith in the information he receives from it. While he is watching the tube, he is told every few minutes, day after day, by mellifluous voices, that this pill or that shampoo can change his life. We worry about the whiteness of our laundry, the shape of our bodies and the sweetness of our breath. Surveys estimate that United States pharmaceutical companies spend billions of dollars each year to promote over-the-counter drugs. Consequently, we are cajoled into buying uppers, downers, vitamins, weight reducers and a hundred other drugs that are incessantly pushed at consumers through the television. Cosmetic companies and detergent manufacturers and breweries employ the same methods. Ideas implanted by commercials affect us all. We eat, drink, dress and make love based on what we see and hear on television, on radio and in print. Literally billions of dollars are spent each year to sell us ideas and products that we could very likely live just as well without. These commercials are actually using the power of suggestion to implant habitual patterns of thinking and behaving among the television audiences.

THE LAWS OF SUGGESTION

Advertisers are well aware of the Laws of Suggestion. These laws are the very ones that Coue' formulated in the early part of the century, and the same ones whose validity was demonstrated by Pavlov's dogs. We demonstrate them constantly ourselves. They are:

I. THE LAW OF CONCENTRATED ATTENTION

This means that when a person concentrates his attention

on an idea, the idea tends to realize itself. An easy-to-understand example of this law is repetitive television and radio advertising. For instance, what do you associate with "the real thing?" How about "You deserve a break today?" Are you guilty of ever feeling "hungry" after a food commercial? How many songs and commercial jingles can you recite that you never consciously memorized? This is also the law which explains how we develop habits (good and bad) and cultivate abilities such as playing a musical instrument or even driving a car.

II. THE LAW OF REVERSED EFFECT

This means that the harder you try to do something, the less chance you have of doing it. When a person thinks he cannot do something and then tries to do it anyway, the more he tries to do it, the less he is able to do it. Most bad habits have one basic thing in common: they grow stronger in the presence of nervous tension.

If I say to you, "Do not think of a purple cow," what is the first thing you think of? I always enjoy demonstrating this law in my classes. I will ask a student to describe a spiral staircase without using his hands. In his effort to keep his hands still, he will actually slightly twirl his head and fidget. He can think of nothing but his perceived need to use his hands to simulate the spiral. This law also applies to the insomniac who tries to go to sleep and to the food or cigarette addict who tries to stop eating or smoking by "reasoning" with his will power. These problems respond to imagination power, not will power. In any battle between the imagination and the will power, it is the imagination that invariably wins—*no exceptions.*

III. THE LAW OF DOMINANT EFFECT

This means that a suggestion is more effective when it is experienced simultaneously with a strong emotion. The suggestion linked with the emotion will displace any other suggestion that is in the mind at that time.

To illustrate, imagine you are walking along a wooded path, enjoying nature and feeling relaxed and peaceful. You glance ahead and see a grizzly bear in the path. The peaceful relaxation you were enjoying would be immediately displaced by stronger emotions of fear. The fear, then, would become the dominant feeling.

Remember that your subconscious mind is a goal-striving, servo-mechanism. It is a goal-directed machine, acting solely on the orders it is given. By its very nature, it seeks success for whatever task you are ordering. It does not have the capacity to distinguish what is real from what is imagined, as we demonstrated earlier with the imagined "lemon."

The strength of the success drive can be illustrated by the following example of how a new skill is learned. You will be able to understand how the Law of Dominant Effect supersedes the Law of Concentration because of the overpowering strength of the success drive.

A person learning to shoot baskets, for instance, will miss the basket many more times than he will hit it. If mere repetition were the answer to improved skill, this practice should make him more expert at missing the basket than at hitting it; that is literally what he practices the most at first. However, although his misses may outnumber his hits ten to one, as he practices, his misses gradually diminish, and his hits come more and more frequently. Why? Simply this: elation and the heady feeling of success are very strong emotions. The subconscious remembers and reinforces his successful attempts, directs the body to "duplicate" the hits, and forget the misses.

When you understand suggestion and its laws, you will

understand all there really is to know about hypnotic induction theory.

A CLASSROOM DEMONSTRATION OF THE LAWS OF SUGGESTION

I enjoy demonstrating all the laws of suggestion in my classrooms by setting up the following scenario.

A student is asked to join me in front of the class. I place him facing me with about ten feet of space between us. I ask the student to look at the floor in front of him and imagine that there is a six-inch-wide plank stretching along the floor from the point where he is to the point where I am.

When he "sees" the plank, I ask him to step carefully forward, and walk across it. This is not usually a problem. The student extends his arms slightly, quickly walks across the "plank" and back again. Then I tell the student, "I want you to imagine now that each of us is on top of an identical ten-story building. The same plank is now stretched between the two buildings. Please walk toward me now."

The change is always startling! The student pauses, "gets the picture," puts both arms all the way out for balance and shakily begins to inch forward. Some go backwards after one step. Others fall off completely. Most teeter about precariously with each step as they walk toward my "building."

What does this prove? The Law of Concentrated Attention allows the student to "see" the plank and the buildings that, of course, aren't there. The Law of Reversed Effect keeps the student from succeeding in walking a plank ten stories high ("I can't really do that, but I'll try"). The Law of Dominant Effect is demonstrated when the stronger emotions of anxiety and fear override the previous feeling of confidence. In each of the above instances, the imagination (what the student pictures in his mind) is in conflict with the will (what the student consciously wants to do). When this happens, as it does with most of us all too frequently, the imagination always, *always* wins.

Properly understood, hypnosis has absolutely nothing to do with "will power." Will power is a function of the conscious mind, whereas the subconscious mind is basically influenced by the imagination.

Regarding this, I again refer to Emile Coué, who made the following observations based on his personal experience of twenty years:

1. In the conflict between the will and the imagination, the force of the imagination is in direct ratio to the square of the will.
2. When the will and imagination are in agreement, one does not add to the other, but one is multiplied by the other.
3. The imagination can be directed.

In other words, when the will and the imagination are working together, the results are not merely the power of one plus the other one. The two working together have the force of one multiplied by the other. He also discovered that we have the power and the ability to direct this awesome force for our benefit . . . through hypnosis.

CHAPTER FOUR

SELF-DEMONSTRATIONS

Are you convinced? Do you believe now that your body follows the orders of your mind?

There are several ways you can easily demonstrate this for yourself. I encourage you to do the following exercises and observe what happens . . .

SELF-DEMONSTRATION #1 Pencil Experiment

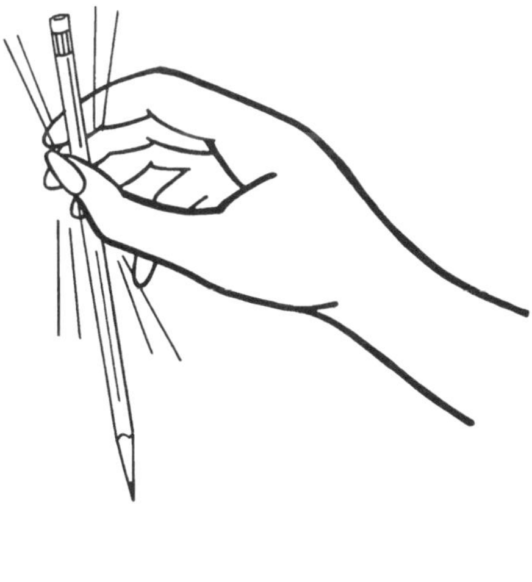

You will need a pencil (or any other object of similar size and shape). Hold it between your thumb and first finger as shown in the illustration. Stare at the pencil intently and say, "I can drop it. I can drop it. I can drop it." Say these words repeatedly with no interruption. During the time you are repeating the sentence over and over in this manner you can try to drop the pencil, but you will find that you can't! In fact, the harder you try to drop it, the tighter your fingers will grasp it. It is impossible for you to drop the pencil if you are thinking the phrase, as instructed, over and over without interruption. This is, of course, another demonstration of The Law of Concentrated Attention. You are saying, "I can", not "I am". Change the words to "I am dropping the pencil", and it happens at once.

SELF-DEMONSTRATION #2 Semaphore Experiment

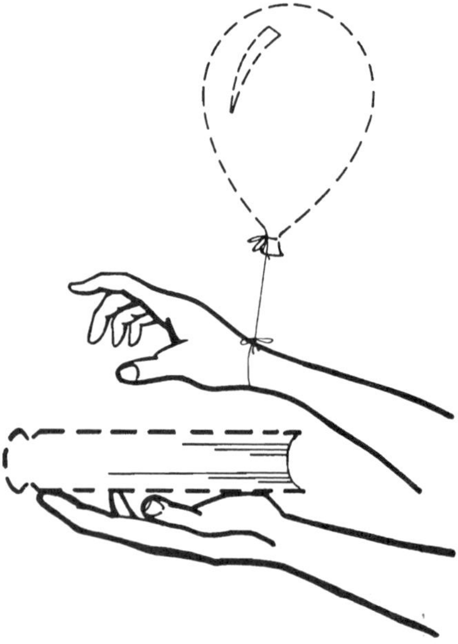

It is important for you to read the instructions completely through before beginning.

Sit comfortably with your feet flat on the floor. Close your eyes, and extend your arms from the shoulders straight in front of you, hands up. Close your eyes and imagine: A large, heavy book has been placed on your left hand. In your mind, your imagination, "see" your hand going down from the weight of the book. "Feel" the book get heavier and heavier as your arm lowers itself with fatigue. On your right wrist is a string with a large helium balloon that is rising to the ceiling. As your right hand responds to being "lifted" by the balloon, it seems to just drift higher and higher. "Feel" the lightness of your arm as you "see" the balloon take your arm even higher. Imagine the color and size of the balloon. Think of your arm as floating upwards.

Concentrate on the images of the heavy book on the left hand and the balloon on the right for a couple of minutes. Just alternate between the two. Then open your eyes.

If you have focused on the images as instructed, you will notice that your right arm is higher than your left arm. The actual distance higher is of no importance. The fact that your imagined "book and balloon" caused a physical reaction is the "proof" that your body carried out the "orders" of your mind.

SELF-DEMONSTRATION #3 The Pendulum

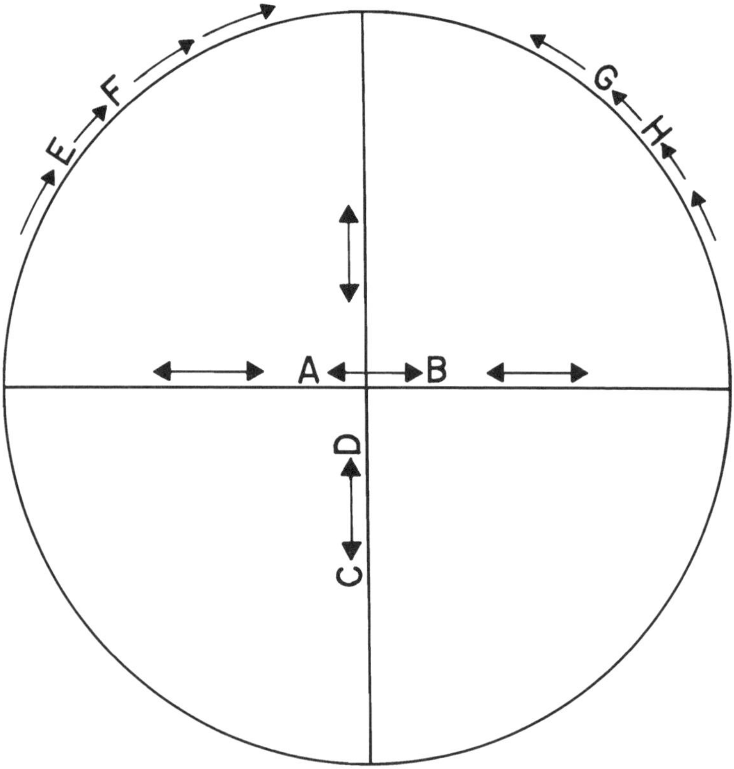

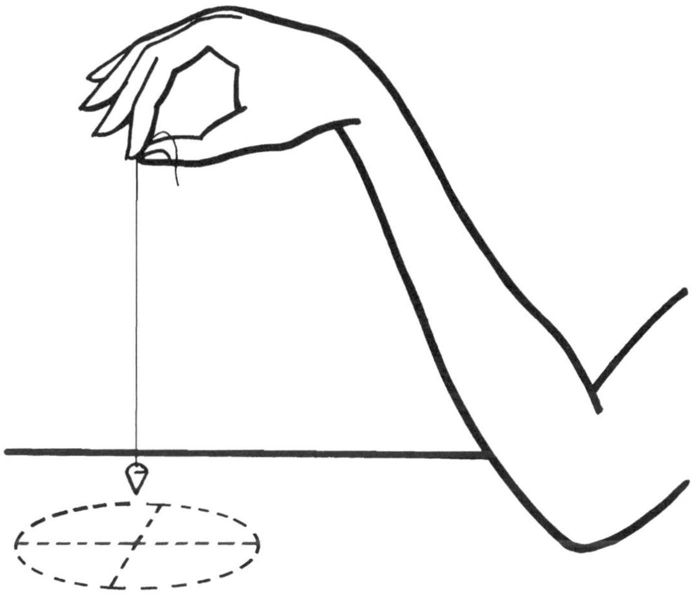

This is everyone's favorite. You will need a pendulum, or you can construct one from a string or ribbon twelve to fifteen inches long with a ring, a washer or a large button tied to the end for weight.

On a plain piece of paper, prepare a visual target as shown in the illustration. The target is simply a circle that has been divided into ninety degree quadrants by two straight lines intersecting in the center. Designate the lines as A ⟷ B and C ⟷ D as shown. The best position for this experiment is sitting at a desk or table with the elbow of the hand you write with resting on the table and the pendulum string held between the thumb and forefinger. Adjust the position of your arm and the point at which you hold the string so that the bottom of the weight is just touching the center of the target with your arm at an angle of 45–60 degrees to the table top as shown in the illustration.

Lift the weight barely off the target (1/4″–1/2″) and think of movement back and forth along either one of the intersecting lines. ("A-B, A-B, A-B" or "C-D, C-D, C-D", etc.) Don't consciously move the string or your hand. Just think on the direction of the line. The pendulum will begin to move in the direction of your thought. Amazing! Stop and start over with a perpendicular motion. Repeat the process with clockwise and counterclockwise motion.

What really happens here? The pendulum is only amplifying tiny muscles in your wrist and fingers in what is called an ideomotor response. Incidentally, the letters used on the intersecting target lines can be called anything—yes, no, north, south, etc., and the results will be exactly the same.

CHAPTER FIVE

THE BRAIN

In hypnotherapy, we are far more interested in the subjective "conscious/subconscious mind" theories than we are in the physical brain. However, it is difficult to literally separate the two.

When we consider the size of the brain (approximately 3 to 3-1/2 pounds), it is almost beyond our comprehension to understand that it contains about a trillion brain cells that control our memory, imagination, communication and health. It is responsible for our most primitive urges and our loftiest ideals. It accounts for the activity of the voluntary and involuntary systems of the body as well as consciousness, perception, thought and creativity.

The brain is made up of many specialized areas or compartments, each with a particular job to do in servicing the body and the thinking processes of the mind.

We know that the neurons in the nervous system are the chemical transmitters of messages from the brain to the body. Everything is controlled from the brain. All thoughts and emotions are transmitted to the cerebral cortex area where they are sorted and analyzed. The thoughts and emotions are received in the form of suggestion from sight, sound, feeling or any combination of the senses. The cortex then transforms the idea of feeling into bodily action.

THE TWO SIDES OF THE BRAIN

As far as physiology is concerned, we only need to know that the human brain has two almost identical halves, both for different functions and responsibilities. The halves are connected and separated by a thick cable containing some 200 million nerve fibers called the corpus callosum.

Although each hemisphere of the brain has its own specialization, and both hemispheres are used by the individual, there is substantial evidence that one or the other of the hemispheres tends to be dominant in each person. Therefore, we are all predominantly "right-brained" or "left-brained".

LEFT HEMISPHERE

The left hemisphere is logical, analytical and rational. It is strongly oriented in reality and controls language and speech. When we are using our left hemisphere, our reasoning is logical and systematic, ordering facts step by step, part by part, one after another, to arrive at one and only one conclusion. For example, "Given numbers *a, b,* and *c*—we can say that if *a* is greater than *b*, and *b* is greater than *c*; therefore, *a* is necessarily greater than *c*." This statement illustrates the left-hemisphere mode: the analytic, verbal, figuring-out, sequential, symbolic, linear, objective mode.

Lawyers, accountants and scientists all have occupations that require logical, sequential and analytical reasoning. For the most part, they are considered "left-brain" people.

RIGHT HEMISPHERE

The right hemisphere is nonrational and intuitive. It is involved with imagination, spatial relationships, music, art and symbolism. It is capable of processing and combining many kinds of information at once, thus allowing it to arrive at hunches or intuitive feelings rather than analytical conclusions. Its reasoning is parallel. We "see" things in this mode of thinking that may be imaginary, or we recall things that are real. We see how things exist in space and how parts go together to make a whole. Using the right hemisphere, we understand metaphors, we dream, and we create new combinations of ideas. When we come across something too complex to describe, we make gestures to communicate more clearly. Using the right hemisphere we are able to draw pictures of our perceptions.

Artists, musicians, writers and poets have occupations that require the synthetic or integrative processing of information. Logic and sequence play little or no part in their day-to-day jobs. They, therefore, are largely "right-brain" individuals.

TWO WAYS OF KNOWING

The concept of the duality, or two-sidedness, of human nature and thought has been taught by philosophers, teachers and scientists from many different cultures and periods. The dominant idea is that there are two distinct, yet parallel "ways of knowing," distinctly correlating to the two sides or hemispheres, of the brain.

These concepts are embedded in our languages and cultures, and they are present in our everyday lives. The main divisions are between thinking and feeling; intellect and intuition; objective analysis and subjective insight. Political comment-ators say that people generally analyze the good and bad points of an issue, and then vote on their gut feelings. The history of our scientific, artistic and technological progress is full of stories of researchers, writers and musicians who try repeatedly to find an answer to a problem, and then have a dream or "flash" in which the answer presents itself. The statement by the nineteenth century mathematician Henri Poincaré is a vivid example of the process:

> One evening, contrary to my custom, I drank black coffee and could not sleep. Ideas rose in crowds; I felt them collide until pairs interlocked, so to speak, making a stable combination ... It seems, in such cases, that one is present at his own unconscious work, made partially perceptible to the overexcited consciousness, yet without changing its nature. Then we vaguely comprehend what distinguishes the two mechanisms or, if you wish, the working methods of the two egos.

In another context, people sometimes say about another person, "The words sound good, but something tells me not to trust her (or him)." Or, "I can't tell you in words exactly what it is, but there is just something about that person that I dislike (or like) very much." Such statements are intuitive observations that both sides of the brain are at work, processing the *same* information in *two different ways.*

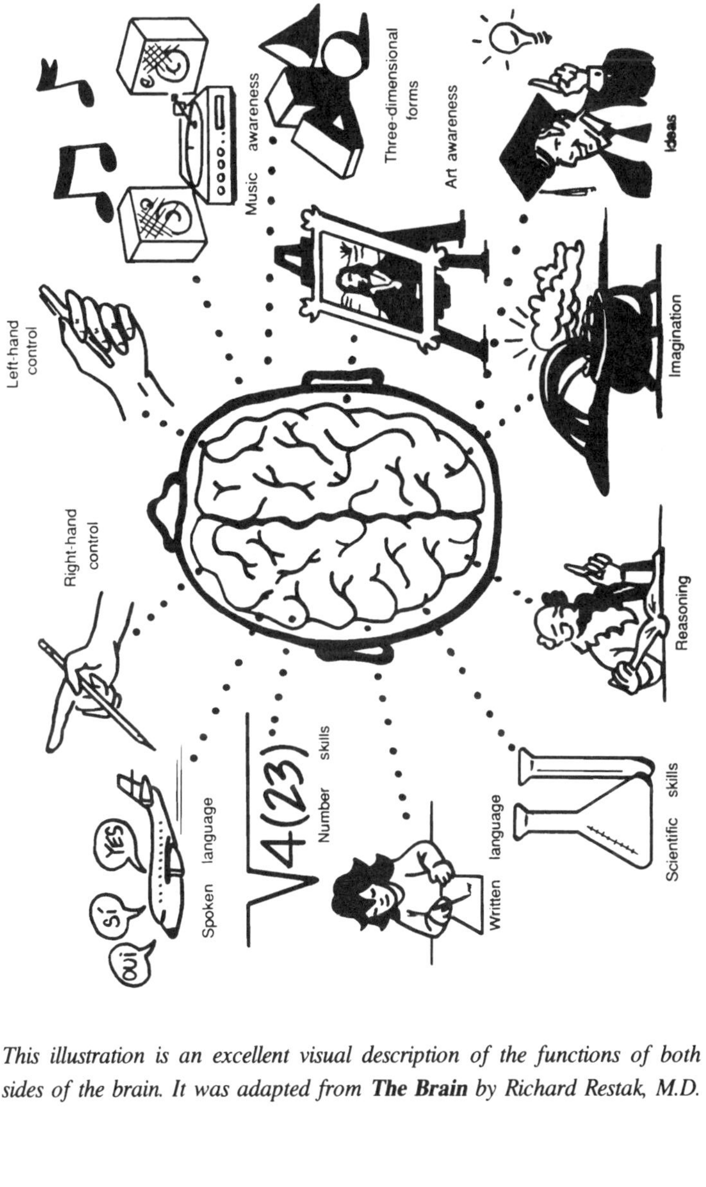

This illustration is an excellent visual description of the functions of both sides of the brain. It was adapted from **The Brain** *by Richard Restak, M.D.*

Anthropologist Thomas Gladwin contrasted the ways that a European sailor and a native Trukese sailor navigate small boats between tiny islands in the vast Pacific Ocean.

Before setting sail, the European begins with a plan that can be written in terms of directions, degrees of longitude and latitude, and estimated time of arrival at separate points on the journey. Once the plan is conceived and completed, the sailor has only to carry out each step consecutively, one after another, to be assured of arriving on time at the planned destination. The sailor uses all available tools, such as a compass, a map, etc., and if asked, can describe precisely how he got where he was going. *The European navigator uses the left-hemisphere mode of thinking.*

Conversely, the island native sailor starts his voyage by imaging the position of his destination relative to the position of other islands. As he sails along, he constantly adjusts his direction according to his awareness of his position thus far. His decisions are improvised continuously by checking relative positions of landmarks, sun, wind direction, etc. He navigates with reference to where he started, where he is going, and the space between his destination and the point where he is at the moment. If asked how he navigates so well without instruments or a written plan, he cannot possibly put it into words. This is not because the islanders are unaccustomed to describing things in words. Rather, it is because the process is too complex and fluid to be put into words. *The Island navigator uses the right-hemisphere mode.*

WHAT KEEPS US FROM USING BOTH SIDES OF OUR BRAINS?

Our culture is generally left-brain dominant because of our emphasis on rational, analytical thinking and verbal expression ability. The focus of our culture has been socio-economic rather than oriented to individual development. As we develop more and more into technological, science-directed industrialized states, we are trained in our schools and colleges in ways that will best serve our economically-based industrial empires. We are educated in ways to survive in the very economic environment that created the schools in the first place.

The structure of our education has, therefore, encouraged us to use only narrow, linear thinking. We generally place less emphasis on creative processes, artistic talent and intuitive thought. Most of our educational system has been designed to cultivate the verbal, rational, on-time left hemisphere, while half of the brain of every student is often neglected.

It has taken centuries to learn about the intricacies of the mind, its abilities and its potential, and we are still exploring what it can do for us. It is heartening to note that in recent years, as we have become more sophisticated and more knowledgeable about the ways of the mind, we have become more aware of the great potential we possess that we have not yet used. By learning to use hypnosis to help us gain access to the vast unused portions of our minds, we are plunging headlong into our capabilities as human beings.

DETERMINING YOUR OWN DOMINANT HEMISPHERE

At this point in my classes I hand out a test that helps the student understand his own right or left brain dominance. I have included it here so that you can take it for yourself. You'll find it enjoyable and maybe even enlightening.

WHICH SIDE OF YOUR BRAIN CALLS THE SHOTS?

Nobody is totally right-brained or left-brained. But just as most people tend to be right-handed or left-handed, they also tend to use one hemispheric mode of thinking over the other. This quiz is designed to help you determine which side of the brain you favor. Once you know, you can begin exercising and building up the strength and participation of your opposite side. If you are already fairly well hemispherically integrated, you'll find it more difficult to choose between the answers in each case. To get the most out of the test, pick the answer that MOST applies to you, the one that is closest to the way you tend to think and act.

1. Think of your favorite song. Close your eyes and let it run through your head for 10 or 15 seconds. Did you focus more on:
   a. the words?
   b. the melody?
2. You're at a restaurant with a friend and he asks you for directions on how to get somewhere. Do you:
   a. draw a map?
   b. write out step-by-step instructions?
3. When you buy audio equipment—a stereo, radio, turntable, or dictaphone—do you:
   a. carefully analyze all the available specifications, data, and statistics, familiarizing yourself with electronic concepts important to the understanding of the spec sheets?
   b. listen to the components in the systems in your price range and pick out one for the quality of the sound and the appearance of the equipment?
4. When you are hung up getting started on a project or working out a problem, is it because:
   a. you get bogged down in all the details, or don't know where to start?
   b. you try to do too many things at the same time and end up with your energies too spread apart, without putting your best abilities to work anywhere?

5. What kind of camera do you prefer:
   a. one that allows you to worry about the picture, and not the camera—an automatic 35, an instamatic, or an instant-developing model?
   b. a manually controlled 35 mm SLR where you have control over the shutter speed, f-stop, flash, etc.?
6.

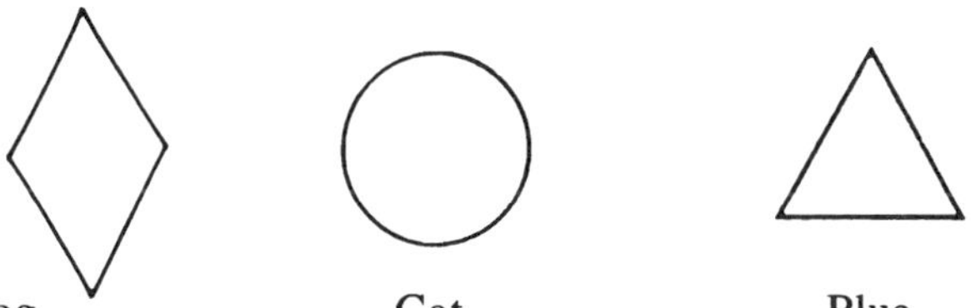

Dog (1)   Cat (2)   Blue (3)

   Does (1) match better with:
   a. (2)?
   b. (3)?
7. Are you sold on an idea:
   a. after carefully reading up on it, analyzing all the aspects step by step?
   b. if you can picture it a success, if it grabs you, or if you can get an intuitive, gut feeling that it will go?
8. Do you tend to judge a person by:
   a. what he says?
   b. his eye contact, body language, and the appearance he presents?
9. When it comes to spectator sports, are you better at:
   a. keeping score, remembering player averages, records, etc.?
   b. mapping out play strategies, anticipating where the action will be?

10.

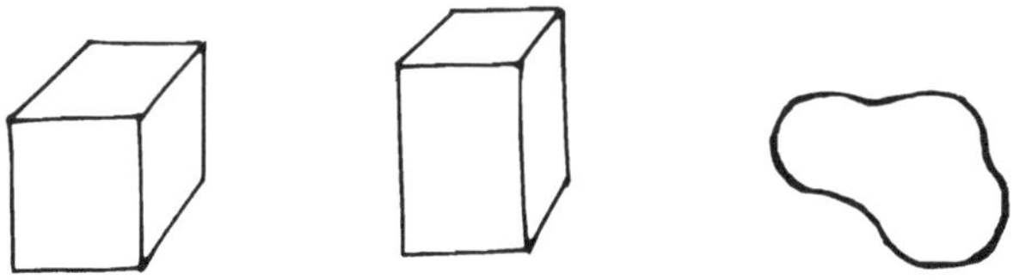

Me (1) — Ear (2) — You (3)

Does (1) match better with:

a. (2)?

b. (3)?

11. Do you work better when:

a. you can do the specialized work that you're best at, analyzing it and making it all add up, without distractions?

b. you can see how your work plugs into the big picture, or if you're involved in interpreting patterns and viewpoints of the whole picture?

12. How do you keep your desk, the place where you work, your hobby room, or garage?

a. It's neat and orderly. Everything has its place. If it gets too cluttered, I can't find anything.

b. It's a mess, but I can find anything I need. If someone should come and clean it up, I'd be lost.

13. Recall what you had for dinner yesterday. Close your eyes and remember for five seconds. Did you:

a. picture in your mind the image, the smells, and tastes of the food you ate?

b. recite a list of the foods the dinner consisted of, using words to describe them?

14. When you buy something to read on your vacation, do you:
    a. take it along and read while others are swimming or sunning themselves?
    b. end up hardly reading it at all because you just let go, loosen up, swim, or soak up the sun?
15. When you work on a project, do you prefer to:
    a. get started right away, as soon as you have a feel for it—diving in and figuring that you can always plug in the gaps later?
    b. have all the facts so that you can analyze them carefully and plan the best sequence of steps for implementing it?
16. When you put something together—like a game, a toy, or a new piece of equipment—do you:
    a. carefully follow the written instructions, step by step, to the letter?
    b. try to eyeball it and figure out on your own how to put it together, maybe just glancing at the instructions when you get stuck?
17. Would you rather describe an object or place by:
    a. writing a complete description?
    b. drawing a simple sketch?
18. Does your mate tend to be more:
    a. logical and analytical, a good talker?
    b. intuitive and emotional, artistic?

19.

(1) Banana | (2) Gun | (3) Peach

Does (1) match better with:

a. (2)?
b. (3)?

Scoring

Give yourself one point for each “a” answer you gave for questions 1, 3, 4, 6, 7, 8, 9, 11, 12, 14, 16, 17, and 18, plus one point for each “b“ answer you gave for 2, 5, 10, 13, 15, and 19.

If you scored 10 or higher, you tend to use a left-hemisphere operating mode-an analytical, verbal, step-by-step approach. You may get hung up on details, or talk yourself into a corner.

If you scored a 9 or less, you are more right-hemisphere oriented. You look for patterns and the big picture. You tend to process information with a visual, spatial, emotional, artistic perspective or approach. Most likely you're a maverick and don't like strict schedules or structured situations that tie you down and restrict you. Your moods have a definite effect on you, and you occasionally will make decisions based on your intuition.

After you've identified your dominant hemispheric mode of thinking, you can improve your attitude and your performance by avoiding the behavior patterns that cause problems for that hemisphere, or by switching to the opposite-hemisphere activities if you find yourself in a rut.

For example, if you are left-brain dominant, not getting anywhere because you get hung up on details, or you've been selling yourself a negative verbal bill of goods, then you can get out of it by engaging in some right-hemisphere activity. Try listening to music, paging through an art or photography book, or taking part in some kind of athletic activity.

If you are right-brain dominant, you can get unstuck from problems (such as not being able to organize yourself) but putting your thoughts down on paper, making outlines, and by analytically dissecting your ideas and objectives in writing.

Ideally, you want to get both halves of your brain working together, rather than overemphasizing either mode. Once you become reintegrated, you'll find yourself functioning more effectively, with more energy and enthusiasm.

Many creative people seem to have an intuitive awareness of the separate-sided brain. For instance, Rudyard Kipling wrote the following poem, entitled "The Two-Sided Man," over fifty years ago:

> Much I owe to the lands that grew—
> More to the Lives that fed—
> But most to the Allah Who gave me Two
> Separate sides to my head.
> Much I reflect on the Good and the True
> In the faiths beneath the sun
> But most upon Allah Who gave me Two
> Sides to my head, not one.
> I would go without shirt or shoe,
> Friend, tobacco or bread.
> Sooner than lose for a minute the two
> Separate sides of my head!
>
> —Rudyard Kipling

HYPNOSIS AND BRAIN WAVES

For many years it has been known that the electromagnetic nature of brain activity can be measured on a device called the electroencephalograph (E.E.G.). The brain produces about ten watts of electrical current. The E.E.G. allows for measurement of the patterns of brain waves. There are four primary brain wave patterns—beta waves, alpha waves, theta waves and delta waves—all of which are contained within a total energy spectrum of 0 to 40 cycles per second (C.P.S.) of vibrations. This brain wave activity has been verified scientifically many times with the use of the E.E.G. machine.

In the last few years, there has been a plethora of publications touting the wonders of "Brain-wave therapy." There are devices which use headphones and earphones to provide the appropriate mixture of electronic light and sound to "synchronize" the right and left hemispheres of the brain. What this tells us is that there is a real possibility that the brain has the ability to change its vibrations, thus affecting not only behavior patterns, but also the involuntary workings of our internal organs. It has been demonstrated countless time in controlled laboratory experiments that in hypnosis, these brain wave changes do occur.

CLASSIFICATION OF BRAIN WAVES

Beta waves. The beta state is one of awakened physical alertness, with the conscious mind alert to all the senses. This is the state in which we spend most of our waking time. It is associated with tension and seeking. It is the critical thought level and is usually associated with such activities as writing a letter, making a shopping list or solving a math problem. Beta waves fall into a fast-paced 14 to 33 vibration C.P.S.

Our average beta level is 21 C.P.S. States of emotion such as pain, anger, fright or joy can cau level to increase to the 30 C.P.S. range. While in beta, we experience a sense of being controlled by time and space.

Alpha waves. The alpha state is one which brings heightened creativity and enhanced physical relaxation. Alpha states produce hypnosis or deep meditation, some subjects referring to it as an "alpha high". The alpha rate of vibration is 8 to 12 C.P.S., and the alpha state is the one most conducive to concentration and new learning. Alpha seems to allow a selective focusing of attention which can include concentration on either a particular point or on a whole range of experiences. Scientific researchers tell us that we all slip in and out of alpha from 5 to 30 times a minute without ever knowing it. This explains how we manage to drive our cars home with no conscious recall of how we got there. It also explains how we can be so engrossed in reading a book or watching a television show that we do not respond to questions asked of us even though at some level, we do "hear" them. Researchers tell us that the alpha state may represent the brain's way of "idling" between states of high mental activity and sleep. While in alpha, we feel detached but alert, experiencing a definite slowing of body pulsation.

Theta waves. In theta consciousness, we are on the brink of nighttime sleep. All of us pass through theta at least twice each day, once in the evening, and again in the morning. Theta waves vibrate at 4-7 C.P.S., and in theta there is control of muscular activities, heart rate and pulse pressure. Scientists, inventors, writers, poets and other creative people often function in this level, depending on the drowsy, reverie state to produce their ideas and solutions.

Delta waves. Delta activity is profound sleep. There is even further slowing down of mental activity (3-7 C.P.S.), and we dream. In the dream state, we sort out our physical and mental processes; it is a period of rest and rejuvenation as well as body cell renewal. Lack of sleep can result in delta deprivation and lead to serious disorders.

HOW WE USE THIS KNOWLEDGE

Attempts have been made to explain hypnosis in physiological terms which can in turn be integrated with the psychological phenomena associated with the hypnotic state.

The various stages of hypnosis—light, medium and deep—have been correlated to the brain wave levels described above. The light stage of hypnosis corresponds to the alpha state. The subject experiences relaxation, serenity, tranquility and focus of attention. A medium state of hypnosis corresponds to the medium to upper levels of theta, while a deep state of hypnosis represents a medium to upper level of theta.

I want to stress here that both the stages of hypnosis and the levels of brain wave activity are constantly fluctuating and overlapping among themselves. Reduced to its fundamentals, it is the job of the hypnotherapist to perpetuate the alpha state, guiding the subject gently into complete relaxation.

HUMAN LEARNING CHANNELS

Just as human beings process information in individual ways (right or left-brain dominant), they also receive information in individual ways. We all receive information via our sense organs, of course, but within the last fifteen years it has been determined that most of us "favor" one sensory system over the others. There is, in fact, a study of human information processing called neuro-linguistic programming (NLP) which goes into immense detail studying and utilizing the subtleties of individual language processing as expressed through the five learning channels: visual, auditory, kinesthetic, olfactory and gustatory.

NLP is fascinating and certainly worthy of further study. However, I do not want to cover it in this book. There are many excellent texts available for you to study as you wish. Check your local library or bookstore for titles. In my opinion, a hypnotherapist who has working knowledge of the three main learning systems can do excellent and effective work.

Therefore, for our purposes here, we will classify all people as being *dominantly* one of the following:

- VISUAL
- AUDITORY
- KINESTHETIC

Visual refers to the sense of sight. Auditory refers to the sense of hearing. Kinesthetic refers to feeling in both an emotional and tactile sense. We all use one of the above as our primary, highly developed system of processing information. Additionally, we all likely use a second system that serves as a strong back-up, and a third which is most likely very weak.

How can you recognize a person's primary system? Watch them, particularly their eye movements; listen to them, particularly to the verbs they use.

HOW TO DISTINGUISH BETWEEN DIFFERENT LEARNING SYSTEMS

Certain words are easier for visuals to understand while other words are clearer to auditories and kinesthetics. If you know someone's primary system, you can tailor your words to match that system. A person's eye movements indicate whether he is "making pictures" (visual), hearing sounds (auditory), or experiencing feelings (kinesthetic).

VISUAL

When a visual person thinks or speaks, his eyes will move up or in some cases stay softly defocused, looking straight ahead. The visual's conversation contains a predominance of visual words. Voice tempo is faster with visuals than with those in the auditory or kinesthetic modes.

Visual people will speak in terms of seeing or watching. Examples: *"I see what you mean". "I can't see that". "Looks good".*

- They will give vivid descriptions of things as though painting a picture.
- They have a tendency to show you something as they're talking . . . will point to something.
- They must have eye to eye contact.

Typically, a visual person will use predicates such as, see, behold, observe, view, witness, look, glance, etc.

AUDITORY

You can recognize an auditory person by observing the way his eyes stay level, moving right and left, or move down and left. Auditories use "sound" words to communicate, and they tend to like the sound of their own voice. Their voices have an even, rhythmic tempo and a melodious, easy-to-listen-to-sound.

Auditory people speak in terms of hearing and sounds. Example: *"Listen to what I have to say". "That sounds good". "Did you hear what happened to ?. . "*

- They make a lot of noise, jingle coins or keys in their pocket, scuffle feet, walk loudly.
- They like to repeat things. If you ask them "What time is it?" they will repeat the question and then give you the answer.

- They laugh at the punch line of a joke and then repeat it.
- They don't need the eye to eye contact that visual people need.

Typically an auditory person speaks using predicates such as listen, hear, take in, hark, attend, etc.

KINESTHETIC

Kinesthetics' eyes move down and right when they are processing information. They readily express feelings about anything; they are lukewarm, they like or hate, they're hot or cold. You will hear "spaces" in a kinesthetic's conversation while he takes time to check out his feelings about what is going on. The kinesthetic's voice is generally deeper than the voices of auditories or visuals.

Kinesthetic people will talk in terms of feeling. Examples: *"I can't get a handle on my life." "I can't grasp that." "I feel like a salad today."*

- They have a tendency to touch a lot, and they have a need to be touched back.
- They touch themselves a lot.

Typically, a kinesthetic person will use predicates such as touch, handle, feel, itch, excite, sharpen, etc.

HOW TO USE THIS KNOWLEDGE WITH HYPNOSIS

What does this have to do with hypnosis? Knowing a person's learning system helps you to communicate more effectively with him, to gain trust and rapport quickly. When you can recognize the similarities and differences between your own primary learning systems and that of someone else, you can alter your responses to that person so that you can communicate more clearly.

To illustrate how this would work in a practical manner, suppose someone is attempting to convey the message, "I know that is true."

A *visually*-oriented person might express that in terms such as, "I know beyond a shadow of a doubt that is true."

An *auditory*-dominant person would say, "Every word of that is true."

A *kinesthetic*-dominant person would say something like, "That is solid information."

Let's try another. The general message is a question, "Do you understand me?"

A *visual's* version of the same thing: "Am I painting a clear picture?"

Auditory: "Does this sound right to you?"

Kinesthetic: "Can you get a handle on this?"

This knowledge is invaluable to the hypnotherapist in his choice of words in formulating suggestions. For instance, if the subject wants to lose weight, there are different ways of expressing that suggestion to him.

If he is primarily a *visual* person, you would say, "Visualize yourself now as you gaze at your reflection in the mirror. See how wonderful you look in your new, attractive clothes."

If he is primarily *auditory*, he would more readily respond to the suggestion, "The sound of your husband's (wife's, friend's, etc.) voice as he compliments you on your slender appearance is music to your ears."

For a primarily *kinesthetic* subject, you would say something like. "How wonderful it feels to know you look your best, and you are in complete control of your appetite."

Using this skill takes some very careful listening and practice on your part, but the results are well worth the effort. You try it. You will be pleasantly surprised at the results.

MODELING, MIRRORING AND PACING

There are several other ways that you can build rapport with your client. The most common ones are *modeling, mirroring* and *pacing.* These techniques are commonly taught in NLP classes, but their existence precedes NLP by many years.

MODELING is probably the most popular and traditional method of working with others. It is simply taking the position you would like the other person to match, speaking to him the way you hope he will respond. For instance, the modeler may be enthusiastic while the other person is depressed, calm while others lose their cool, strong when others falter.

MIRRORING is the technique you employ when you want to show a person that you are on his side, that you are not threatening. A subtle mirroring of another's body movements implies sympathy. Usually people in agreement unconsciously assume the same stance, use the same gestures and move at the same tempo. If your client is agitated, depressed, defensive, or tense, you should ally yourself with him by assuming the same position and mannerisms, very slightly, of course. After you have established rapport with that person, you can begin to very slightly change your posture and your mannerisms to a more positive position, and guess what? Your client will follow you and unconsciously begin to change his postures and mannerisms to match yours.

Verbal mirroring is more complex. You can be quite effective if you concentrate on the tone and tempo of your client's voice. Do your best to match it, and watch the profound results.

PACING, to quote the eminent Milton Erickson, means "... meeting people where they are by reflecting what they know or assume to be true or by matching some part of their ongoing experience." Pacing is used in concert with modeling and mirroring, and, more simply put, allows you to voluntarily enter your client's world for a brief moment for the purpose of leading him toward his stated goal. One way to do this is to ask questions that can only be answered, "Yes," or whatever other response you desire. This is demonstrated fully in Chapter Nine on my therapeutic techniques.

Find out your own primary learning system by going over the following checklist that I use in my classes. Make a check mark beside each one of the descriptive phrases that you think applies to you. The category with the most check marks is your primary learning channel. The one with the second highest number of checks is your secondary learning channel. You will probably find that you do not have very many checks in one category, while the two others may be very close. There is no "right" or "wrong" way to score on this. It is only an indicator that is meant to be a communications tool.

CHECKLIST FOR DISCOVERING LEARNING SYSTEMS

STRONG IN AUDITORY CHANNEL

1. Prefers to have someone else read instructions when putting a model together.
2. Reviews for a test by reading notes aloud or by talking with others.
3. Talks aloud when working a math problem.
4. Prefers listening to a cassette over reading the same material.
5. Commits Zip Code to memory by saying it.
6. Uses rhyming words to remember names.

7. Plans the upcoming week by talking it through with someone.

8. Prefers oral instructions from an employer.

9. Likes to stop at a service station for directions in a strange city.

10. Prefers talking/listening games.

11. Keeps up on news by listening to the radio.

12. Is able to concentrate deeply on what another person is saying.

13. Uses free time for talking with others.

STRONG IN VISUAL CHANNEL

1. Likes to keep written records.

2. Typically reads billboards while driving or riding.

3. Puts model together correctly using written directions.

4. Follows written recipes easily when cooking.

5. Reviews for a test by writing a summary.

6. Writes on napkins in a restaurant.

7. Can put a bicycle together from a written instruction.

8. Commits a Zip Code to memory by writing it.

9. Uses visual images to remember names.
10. Is a bookworm.
11. Plans the upcoming week by making a list.
12. Prefers written directions from an employer.
13. Prefers to get a map and find own way in a strange city.
14. Prefers reading/writing games like SCRABBLE.

STRONG IN TOUCH/MOVEMENT CHANNEL

1. Likes to build things.
2. Uses sense of touch to put a model together.
3. Can distinguish items by touch when blindfolded.
4. Learns touch system rapidly in typing.
5. Moves with music.
6. Doodles and draws on any available paper.
7. Is an out-of-doors person.
8. Moves easily; is well coordinated.
9. Spends a large amount of time on crafts and handiwork.
10. Likes to feel texture of drapes and furniture.

11. Prefers movement games to games where one just sits (may be a function of age).

12. Finds it fairly easy to keep fit physically.

13. One of the fastest in a group to learn a physical skill.

14. Uses free time for physical activities.

THE STRESS DECADES LEAD US INTO THE MIND

As our culture made rapid strides in the early part of the century and into the 70's, we speedily advanced into areas beyond the comprehension of most people. We saw the harnessing and releasing of atomic energy, the advent of computers, the march into space, and countless other great technological advances. However, as with all great accomplishments, there was a great price. The price was inner peace. We gave new meaning to the word "stress," and rather than turning to ourselves to cope with the new era, we turned to tranquilizers, pills, and a variety of new cults and mystic religions. We used our minds less and outside intervention more.

For a few, the 1960's and 70's became a time to probe the mind, and a quiet cultural revolution began. People became dissatisfied with the paths of the past, and they began looking for new ways to understand themselves, new ways of coping. The mind was the key. The hope was for a link to a better understanding of life and how to survive, even excel, within the boundaries of the new technological society. People began testing the boundaries that had been established by society. It was a turbulent, trying time that left memories of discord and discontent. Perhaps the most beneficial aspect of that period was the beginning of our probe inward into the mind to find the solutions.

As we leave the 80's, we are just now realizing that our most valuable legacy from those confusing years is the knowledge that we can turn to ourselves for answers . . . and to stop seeking temporary relief from outside sources, probing inward to our minds instead.

CHAPTER SIX

THE CONSCIOUS AND SUBCONSCIOUS MIND

The human mind is a fascinating, remarkable instrument. It is both a collector and storer of information; it is also the controller of our physical and mental functions. An entire lifetime could easily be spent studying and investigating the mind, and there would still be more to learn.

YOUR MIND IS MORE THAN A BRAIN

It is important for you to know that your mind is more than just a brain. You are an information processing system made up of all your neural systems and every cell and part of your body.

Your mind is highly efficient and highly complex in its functioning. Mankind with all of its advanced technology and resources, has never been able to create anything that compares with it.

The many talents of the multi-part human mind are most apparent in the area of language. Most five-year-olds have mastered the general syntax and idiosyncrasies of their native language, but multimillion-dollar computers remain stumped in that area. Computers have trouble recognizing misspelled words, filling in incomplete sentences or understanding regional speech variations. Yet all of us do this many times each day, often at a nearly unconscious level when our conscious minds are considering other incoming information. A simple, almost automatic human activity like getting dressed or washing a car would involve trillions of bits of information in a computer program. Nothing that man's mind has invented can compare with the mind itself. We must not lose sight of the fact that it was the human mind that created all of the wonderful electronic technology that we enjoy today, not the reverse.

A FEW FACTS ABOUT THE MIND

The largest computer assembled to date is reported to have over 100 million connections in its complicated electronic memory system. Each of these connections is an attempt to electronically duplicate the functions of one single human brain cell, the neuron. Consider now that each human brain has over 10 to 15 billion connections and neurons. This being so, it would take literally a thousand or more of these giant man-made computers to equal the capacity of a single human brain. Additionally, the human brain contains a supportive system of 50 to 80 billion neuroglia cells which serve as backups to the neurons.

HOW THE MIND PROCESSES INFORMATION

The mind processes information in two distinct ways:

1. It heeds, takes notice. *What is this? What's happening here? What shall I do about it?*

2. It acts, responds. It sends out orders that move the body into action by sending messages to other parts of the system. These messages, chemical, electrical and mechanical, are given on both the *conscious* and the *subconscious* level.

While science still has much to learn about the human mind's complexities, there is some information that is generally accepted as fact. We know that the mind functions on two levels or in two principle areas, namely, the *conscious* mind, where it is estimated that we function at the 10 percent level, and the *subconscious* mind, where 90 percent of our mind function occurs.

You have undoubtedly heard many times before that we only use 10 percent of our minds. This is no new-age-thinking jargon; it is a physiological fact.

The brain's neurons are connected to each other by connective bridges forming a complex network. Scientists have estimated that only about 10 percent of the available neuron connections are ever used by the majority of human beings. This ten percent is the *conscious* mind. More and more neurons can be brought into this great system by using the other 90 percent of the mind, the magnificent *subconscious* part, thereby tapping into the enormous information processing capabilities of the brain to a much greater extent.

These two areas of mind directly correlate with the two hemispheres of the brain. The conscious, "thinking" mind functions primarily in the left brain, while the subconscious, "feeling" mind functions primarily in the right brain. This two-fold nature of mind activity does not indicate two minds or even one mind operating with two separated, segregated divisions. It indicates, instead, an interrelated process when the conscious and subconscious, or left- and right-brain activity is simultaneous.

It has become apparent to scientists that both sides of the brain and both levels of consciousness require the use of specific procedures and techniques if they are ever to be used to their fullest potential. Hypnosis allows us the opportunity to do this.

THE CONSCIOUS AND SUBCONSCIOUS MIND AT WORK

Imagine that you are spending the day at a large amusement park such as Disneyland. You are eager and enthusiastic as your *conscious* mind takes in all of the exciting sights, sounds and smells. You are thoroughly enjoying the wonderful and thrilling surroundings.

You notice the people. You admire the flowers. You smell the popcorn and the many kinds of food at the concession stands. You are actively and *consciously* occupied with such questions as, "What ride should I try next?, I wonder if that one will be too rough?, I wonder where those people are from?, What shall I eat for lunch?, I wonder if the lines will be shorter this evening?, etc., etc."

Meanwhile, your new, tight-fitting shoe is rubbing your foot, and your *subconscious* mind is absorbed in sending out the messages to your body to form a protective blister around that irritated area of your foot.

Only after the blister is formed, and the sensation of pain in the foot registers with the *conscious* mind, does your *conscious* mind redirect its attention to the pain: "What shall I do about this blister?"

Suddenly the focus of conscious attention is switched from the thrill of the amusement park and the lure of the attractions to a new priority: the blistered foot!

THE CONSCIOUS MIND

"Consciousness" means awareness. When you are conscious

of something, you know it, are aware of it. I once heard a story of a philosophy student who asked his professor the following question: "How do I know that I am?" The professor inquired, "Who is asking?" The fact is that you are, because you are aware . . . are conscious. Your conscious mind knows of your body and your surroundings. This knowledge, this consciousness, is achieved through your sense organs. You can take the information received through your sense organs and use it to think, form judgments and make decisions. Your conscious mind enables you to do these things by breaking down the information into small parts. It then analyzes, makes comparisons, evaluates, reasons and finally forms a response to the presenting problem. You also use your conscious mind to control all voluntary bodily movements, so when you speak, open and close your eyes, run, sit, write, etc., you use your conscious mind. It takes the information you used and stores it in the unlimited recesses of your subconscious mind. The information stored there serves as a basis for your future actions and decisions.

THE CONSCIOUS MIND SELECTS AND DISCRIMINATES

Your conscious mind draws upon this stored information constantly in order to meet your day-to-day needs. It allows you to make decisions and exercise the power of choice. It gives you the ability to select and discriminate between what is desirable and what is not. For example, if you begin to feel cold, your conscious mind refers to prior experiences stored in your subconscious memory and obtains the different alternatives you know from previous experience to become warm, such as, put on a sweater, go inside, light a fire, move around, etc. You can then decide your choice of action.

You act upon that decision and once again, the information

is added to your subconscious memory banks. When you sleep, your conscious mind recedes, and your subconscious mind takes over. However, if while you are sleeping an emergency occurs such as a fire, a sick child, an intruder, etc., your conscious mind takes over again, and you respond appropriately. This is possible because your senses are always functional, and they are controlled by your conscious mind.

To summarize, we know that the conscious mind is:

1. Characterized by awareness. The very fact of being aware is confirmation that the conscious mind is dominant and in control.
2. In contact with reality. All of the sense organs—for touch, taste, vision, hearing and smell—report to the conscious mind. The reality of our bodies and our environment comes to us through these sense organs.
3. A gatherer of information. It is also through the sense organs that all manner of information is observed and gathered.
4. A sorter of information. The information observed and gathered through the sense organs must be manipulated and sorted for it to be retrieved to meet our needs. This is one of the ways we think.
5. A probability tester. By exploring the probability of certain events happening, it can make decisions about which actions to take in any given circumstance. This is another form of thinking.
6. A decision maker and judge. After examining the possibilities and probabilities, exploring the alternatives and options, the conscious mind makes a judgment. It then selects and directs actions accordingly.
7. A presenter of information to the subconscious. Whatever conclusions are reached as a result of the experience selected are presented by the conscious mind to the subconscious mind for storage in the memory bank.

8. A retriever of information from the subconscious. In order to meet the needs defined by the sense organs, the conscious mind draws constantly from the memory bank deep in the subconscious mind.

The conscious mind functions largely in the left hemisphere of the brain.

HOW THE CONSCIOUS MIND THINKS

The conscious mind thinks in two ways: *inductively* and *deductively.*

INDUCTIVE THINKING

When making a diagnosis, a medical doctor thinks inductively. For example, imagine that a mother has brought in her small child for an examination because the child has a high fever and a rash with blisters that seems to be spreading. The doctor makes a mental note of those two facts. Additionally, the doctor notices that the child is scratching at the rash and has a slight runny nose. He asks about the rash and the runny nose, and he learns that they have both been present for a day or two.

After making all of his observations, the doctor determines that the child has chicken pox. He arrived at his decision by an inductive thinking process. This is the process by which we observe a number of particulars, and arrive at a general conclusion.

DEDUCTIVE THINKING

Imagine now that the mother takes her child home, and

she reports to the school that her child is ill. She tells the teacher that the child has chicken pox. When the teacher explains to the class what chicken pox is, she must describe the symptoms to them. She tells them that chicken pox is characterized by fever, rash, itching, etc. The teacher must use deductive thinking in order to make this explanation. She must think from the general (chicken pox) to the particular (symptoms).

THE SUBCONSCIOUS MIND

Your subconscious mind consists of associated sense impressions and memories of all your past. It is composed of your brain, your spinal cord and a network of nerves that branch out through your entire body. These nerves extend from head to toe, and information about your every move, every thought and every emotion follows the route from your brain to the area of your body concerned. Every single bodily activity is thus controlled. This includes the involuntary internal organs, such as those that make up your digestive, circulatory, reproductive and respiratory system, as well as every physical motion, down to the blinking of an eye. Your subconscious mind controls the health and function of every cell of every organ, bone tissue, etc., that is contained in your body. Every automatic habit and personal idiosyncracy you have is controlled by your subconscious mind.

Subconscious activity is a function of the right hemisphere of the brain.

This subconscious communication goes on day and night, whether you are awake or asleep. Your subconscious mind is dominant when you sleep; it is always active. It maintains a storage bank of memories that include everything that ever happened to you—every experience, relationship, word spoken—everything.

Not only are the memories of your every experience, good and bad, stored in your subconscious mind, but also therein are the memories of the emotions and the environment that accompanied the experience.

YOUR SUBCONSCIOUS REMEMBERS EVERYTHING

One of the most popular sections of my hypnotherapy classes is the age regression demonstration in which I will ask a hypnotized adult student to recall his first grade experience. He will not only recall his teacher's name and description, he will also fully describe the children in his class. He will call his classmates by name, and tell you who were his favorites and why. He knows where he sat, where the pencil sharpener was, where the coats were hung, and where the cafeteria was located. He will often respond in a child-like voice as he stumbles through the alphabet, and he will "draw" his name in block letters, as he did in the first grade! When he is brought out of hypnosis he is amazed to find that memories of that time and its experiences continue to come to him—things he thought he had long forgotten.

Your subconscious mind controls all the functions of your body which are not under direct control of your conscious mind, and upon specific occasions it actually takes over the powers of the conscious mind. For example, the subconscious mind can prevent the conscious mind from speaking, resulting in stuttering or stammering.

THE SUBCONSCIOUS IS A PROBLEM-SOLVER

It is also known that the subconscious is the seat of your dreams and that some dream content is the effort of your subconscious to search out improvement solutions for your life. It can, and does, in fact have the ability to solve problems. How many times have you heard someone say, "I don't know right now. Let me sleep on it." The subconscious mind works on that particular problem overnight, and in the morning, the person seems to have a fresh approach, a new perspective, or the sought-after solution. Within the subconscious is also inspiration and invention. Many creative geniuses describe how they review a problem in consciousness before retiring, knowing that during sleep their subconscious will search out possibilities and present them with an answer.

There are numerous examples of creative work accomplished by men who moved through their activities with leisure and balance, relying solely on the knowledge that at the proper time, their subconscious minds would serve up the right answers for them.

The scientist Alfred Russell Wallace would go for weeks feeling no desire for or interest in his work. During these periods he occupied himself with his garden or simply by reading a novel. Then, a sudden impulse would come bringing him an explanation, a theory, a discovery or a plan, usually like "a flash of light." Thomas Edison did most of his creative work at night, and has been quoted as saying, "my ideas leaped out of my dreams." He was well-known for the many catnaps he took during the day, always with a pad and pencil beside his bed. Henry Cobb, millionaire businessman, once said that all of the really important ideas which helped him to build his business arrived in his mind at night while lying in bed. The great Frenchman, Voltaire, frequently spent as much as fifteen hours in bed, calling his secretary at all hours when there was anything to be committed to writing.

The historical documentation of great masterpieces of literature, art and music is full of such examples of subconscious revelations. The roster of famous people who have changed the course of history by using some form of mental programming covers every field of accomplishment. As I pointed out in the previous chapter, The Brain, exploration of the documentation of our civilization proves that the most significant discoveries, the most creative material, and the most rewarding insights emerged from subconscious activity during moments of relaxation and rest.

THE SUBCONSCIOUS IS A SERVO-MECHANISM

Remember that the subconscious mind is a servo-mechanism. By definition, a servo-mechanism is a machine, so constructed that it automatically "steers" its way to a goal, a target or an answer. The subconscious mind has neither emotion nor opinion. It responds only from the information stored within its memory, retrieving that information very much as you would pull up a letter from a file cabinet. It accepts uncritically all suggestions and ideas given to it by the conscious mind, and it acts upon them with no judgment whatsoever. It cannot differentiate between what is real and what is imagined. No amount of will power exerted by the conscious mind can override it for any extended time. That is why you salivated when you thought of a lemon. That is also why hypnosis works. The relaxed state of hypnosis provides easier access to your subconscious mind. (See Illustration.)

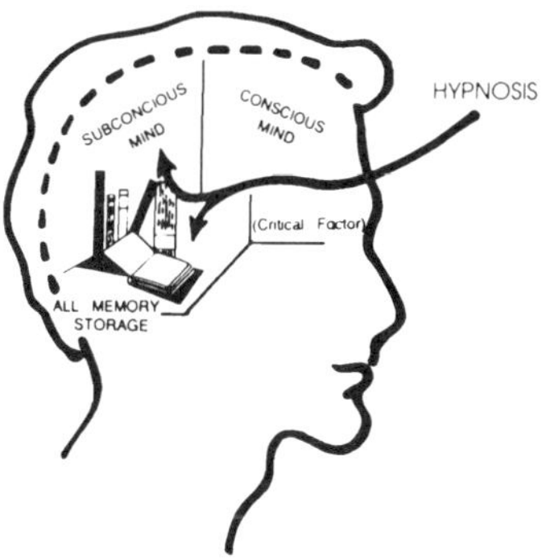

The servo-mechanism or computer-like subconscious mind can be programmed, or re-programmed, to change habits and attitudes . . . to change your life.

HOW THE SUBCONSCIOUS THINKS

Unlike the conscious mind which can think both inductively and deductively, the subconscious mind can think only inductively, that is, from the particular to the general. It must draw its information from the stored experiences, opinions and general conclusions placed there over the years by the conscious mind, and come to a decision to act based on that information.

If you ask a small child what happens to naughty children, he will give you particulars based on his own experience and observation of what he has come to believe such children deserve. The same process occurs when an adult is asked any general question. What do you think about the space program? Would a man or woman be better for that job? What would happen if we expanded our business? All of the answers to questions like this require that the person draw on his prior impressions, memories and sensory experiences in order to come up with an answer.

WATCH A MOVIE, UNDERSTAND YOUR MIND

Have you seen a good movie lately? I recently rented the video of an old favorite of mine, *Chariots of Fire*. My personal experience with this movie is a good illustration of what I've been saying about the actions and reactions of the conscious and subconscious minds. The movie is set in 1924 and is about two Olympic competitors. Near the end of the film, we watched the 100-meter dash. Because of the events leading up to that point, it was a very exciting time. As the character Harold, played by actor Ben Cross, dug in for the start, my own heart began to pound; with the sound of the gun my heart beat even faster, and my fists clenched as I leaned forward in my chair. When Harold crossed the finish line and broke through the tape, I at once felt a tremendous sense of relief and happiness. I was completely swept up in the excitement of the crowd as they rushed onto the field.

What was happening? Simply this: While watching the movie, I experienced parts of it as real. The intensity of that reality was manifested in my sincere emotional responses, my pounding heart and the physical movement of my body in concert with what was happening on the screen. To use a vernacular expression, I was really "into" the movie.

Now, I'm sure you have had a similar experience many times. You were watching a movie or a play. Consciously, you were watching actors and actresses on a screen or stage, but no matter. Unconsciously, you were transported to another world, and your body responded accordingly. Yes, you were hypnotized. You probably just didn't know it.

In hypnosis you are directed into an identical state . . . only the "screen" is inside your mind, and the "movie" is the imagery you create of the new, improved you.

CHAPTER SEVEN

FORMULATING SUGGESTIONS

It has been said many times that suggestion is the very heart of hypnosis. As I mentioned earlier in Chapter Three, if you understand suggestion, you really understand all you need to know about hypnotic induction theory. Technically, a suggestion is a recommendation for belief and action that is accepted by the subconscious mind.

The subconscious mind lacks the critical awareness of the conscious mind, so suggestions must be expressed in a positive way. This is true whether you are working as a therapist with another person as your subject or with yourself in self-hypnosis (which is covered in a later chapter). Remember, with no critical faculty to appraise suggestions, the subconscious is very literal in its interpretations.

The subconscious does not deal with implications or innuendos. For instance, if you ask a hypnotized person, "Can you tell me where you were born?," he will probably answer, "Yes." The subconscious will answer the question as it is posed. In contrast, the conscious mind will answer the same question with the location only, automatically making the necessary assumptions to come up with the answer that the inquirer was really seeking, "Chicago." When addressing the subconscious mind, a better way to ask the question would be, "Where were you born?" For this reason, the hypnotherapist must also make his suggestions direct and straightforward.

BASIC RULES FOR FORMULATING SUGGESTIONS

Everything you have learned about the Laws of Suggestion, human learning systems and the subconscious mind should influence you in your formulation of suggestions. Additionally, there are five rules to remember when choosing the words that will become a hypnotic suggestion:

1. BE POSITIVE
2. BE SPECIFIC
3. BE REALISTIC
4. BE REPETITIVE
5. USE PRESENT-TENSE VERBS

BE POSITIVE

Carefully worded, positive suggestions will demonstrate the benefits to be enjoyed by following them. They should persuade, not command; the subconscious must be seduced into believing. That can be accomplished only through properly prepared suggestions. The subconscious is eager to comply very literally with directives it believes to be true and in your best interests. It follows then, that negative words have no place in therapeutic suggestions. The subconscious is far too literal. There are some words that you should virtually eliminate from your "hypnotic vocabulary". Such words include:

- can't
- never

- pain
- hurt
- try
- perhaps
- angry

The word "try", for instance, presupposes doubt. If the therapist tells the subject to "try" to relax, the Law of Reverse Effect comes into play and says, "The harder you try, the less you can do it." A more effective way of wording that particular suggestion is, "You are beginning to relax," or, "You feel so relaxed."

Your suggestions must be goal-oriented and speak of success. Learn to focus on the desired result. Do not mention or otherwise acknowledge the undesirable difficulty.

POSITIVE VS. NEGATIVE SUGGESTIONS

Let's look at the following two suggestions, both for alleviation of in "test jitters":

incorrect:

A. You will not *tense-up* or *become nervous* when taking your examinations.

correct:

B. During examinations you are *always calm, relaxed* and *composed,* and whatever you have learned *flows freely and easily* through your mind.

Notice the word "not" in A. Watch out for words like not, no, never, can't, won't, don't, etc. They are sure signals that you are formulating negative suggestions. Notice also the words "tense-up" and "nervous" in A. These words describe the failure mechanism or undesirable behavior. They serve no purpose except to concentrate on the problem.

Now look at B. There are no negative words in the sentence, and such words as "calm", "relaxed", "composed", and "easily" refer only to success, with no mention of the negative traits you are seeking to eliminate. In B, the entire direction is toward the goal.

Here are a few more contrasting suggestions to study:

incorrect:

A. You will have *no difficulty* in falling asleep at night, and you wake up in the morning with an *unclouded mind, not feeling tired* at all.

correct:

B. When you are ready to retire at night, you fall asleep *easily and effortlessly* and awaken in the morning *feeling refreshed and full of vim and vigor.*

incorrect:

A. You are *no longer bored* all the time.

correct:

B. You are *energetic and alert,* interested in everything.

incorrect:

A. You are *not self-conscious or afraid.* Your voice does not quiver.

correct:

B. You are a *relaxed, posed* presenter, *pleased with your performance.*

See the difference? Watch out for negative words and words which allude to failure. Concentrate completely on the desired end result. What the mind sees, the body will tend to do.

BE SPECIFIC AND DETAILED

The subconscious mind loves adjectives and descriptive phrases. Choose words that depict clear and vivid images, words that evoke emotion and excitement. Examples of such words:

- radiant
- vibrant

- wonderful
- delightful
- thrilling
- sparkling
- bright

Analyze the goal of the therapy, and structure the suggestions to cover every detail of the desired change.

For example, in formulating suggestions for improved public speaking, saying only, "You are an excellent speaker," simply isn't enough. The following is more appropriate, and will be much more effective: **"You like people. You enjoy the company of other people. You are wonderfully at ease with other people. You especially enjoy talking to them. When you stand before an audience, you are filled with self-confidence and warmth toward the people you are addressing. You are poised and calm. Your gestures are spontaneous and relaxed. You are secure and confident as you speak, and your vibrant enthusiasm makes you a delightful presenter."**

BE REALISTIC

Make the goal appealing enough to provide incentive, but not so dramatic that it seems impossible. Obviously, a struggling student who needs help with study habits is not likely to win the Nobel Prize for literature next month. A mother of four small children will not have a perfectly calm, organized day every day. Discussion or consideration of changes that are clearly unrealistic is not only a waste of time, but it is also a disservice to your client.

If the desired result is one that can be measured such as a sales figure, a specific body weight or a tennis score, include that in your suggestion. You do not need to set a rigid schedule of behavior modification, but you should indicate, within reasonable limits, the time within which you expect the behavior change to occur. If you want to designate immediate action, use the words, "in a moment," or "now," or "in just a short while." If, for instance, relaxation is the goal, you can say, **"In a moment you will find that you are more relaxed than you've ever been before."** If the therapeutic goal is a longer-term effort, you will need to say, **"When you are at the dinner table with your family tomorrow, you will be pleased to notice that you are satisfied with healthy, reasonable portions of food."**

Be certain that your suggestions can be interpreted literally. If you suggest to a football player that he will "tackle like a bull" in the next football game, he could possibly go out playing on all fours!

Structure your suggestions to make the change within the person, not to others. Do not say, "Your co-workers always admire and respect you." Instead, you might say, **"You are interested in your co-workers, and you understand their point of view. You express your respect for their opinions because you value them as human beings. You are confident in your own abilities, and your attitude radiates security and comfort."**

Do not describe abilities. Instead, describe actions that depict abilities. "You have the ability to be your firm's top salesperson," for example, is a remote and nonspecific suggestion. A more realistic and believable alternative is: **"Your new habits of making three new contacts each day and consistently showing positive enthusiasm makes you a valuable, productive salesperson."**

BE REPETITIVE

Repetition is important because it helps to strengthen the suggestion and aid in its retention. Remember The Law of Concentrated Attention? As a suggestion is repeated and accepted, its acceptance becomes assured, and positive actions upon it become natural and effortless. It does not matter what the nature of the suggestion is; you can repeat it in several ways by a slight change in wording. For example, if you are giving a suggestion to lose weight, you can overtly repeat, **"You are satisfied with just enough food to meet your body's nutritional needs, you are satisfied with just enough food to meet your body's nutritional needs, you are satisfied with just enough food to meet your body's nutritional needs, etc."**

An alternative to the overt repetition is to slightly change the key expression. **"You are satisfied with just enough food to meet your body's nutritional needs. You find that you feel full with small portions of healthy food. You enjoy the feeling of eating good food in limited quantities."**

The words can be changed in an infinite number of ways. In this particular situation, your singular therapeutic purpose is to provide a strong, positive acceptable suggestion that will result in the modification of a person's eating habits and enable him to lose weight.

USE PRESENT-TENSE VERBS

Speak of the desired goal as already accomplished. Do not refer to past situations, even for comparison's sake. "You are calmer now than you were last week." Such a suggestion presents a confusing dual image to the subconscious. You can see that "calmer now" and "than you were last week" are two entirely different images. The literal subconscious will only accept one. Last week's condition has been *experienced* and is already stored in the subconscious memory bank of the individual ... it is more real to the subconscious and therefore more likely to be accepted.

Likewise, speaking of future events is a questionable thing to do unless there is a specific goal date. Words like "someday" or even "very soon" are meaningless and vague. When there is a specific future date or event, mention it, but keep the action in the present. For instance, if the subject is a student who is seeking relief from anxiety before a final exam, say, **"Visualize yourself taking your test next month, calm and relaxed as *you answer* the questions easily from the knowledge you have gained from your studies."**

Another time that it is suitable to speak in terms of the future is when the concern is a physical condition. If a person is immobilized with a sprained ankle, **"Your ankle is strong and healthy"**, will obviously not be accepted by the subconscious. A more realistic, appropriate suggestion is, **"Each day your ankle grows stronger and healthier."**

STYLES OF SUGGESTIONS

We learned earlier of the many different ways we receive suggestions in everyday life. So, too, must we alter the style of *giving* suggestions to most effectively benefit the subject. There are many styles of suggestions, the most common being *authoritative* and *permissive.* Additionally, there are *deepening suggestions, imagery suggestions* and *posthypnotic suggestions.* This may sound confusing at first, but all of these types of suggestions are nothing more than ways for you to meaningfully communicate with the subconscious mind.

AUTHORITATIVE OR PERMISSIVE?

In the conversation before hypnosis, the hypnotherapist decides whether to use an *authoritative* or *permissive* style.

AUTHORITATIVE SUGGESTIONS are designed to instruct a certain response, simply and to the point. An example of an authoritative suggestion for relaxation is, *"Breathe deeply, and as you exhale, feel all the muscles in your body begin to relax".*

If the subject is in any profession where he is accustomed to following orders, or is employed in a subordinate position by the military or police, the direct, authoritative suggestion is most likely to be the style of choice. Other indicators for the use of the authoritative style of suggestion can be observed as you talk with your client. Does he unhesitatingly take a seat where you ask him to? Does his posture indicate "readiness" to respond? Does he openly react to simple pleasantries, allowing rapport to naturally develop? Does he nod frequently and indicate his willingness to "take your word" for whatever you say? These are all signs of a person who will respond nicely to the authoritative approach.

PERMISSIVE SUGGESTIONS convey the same thought as the authoritative suggestion, but the desired response is presented only as a possibility, a natural consequence of something you are encouraging rather than directing, such as, *"As you allow yourself to become more relaxed, you may begin to observe your breathing as it becomes deeper and more regular. If you take a deep breath and exhale slowly, you may notice how your muscles seem to want to relax . . ."*

If the subject seems wary, analytical or is in a profession where he is used to giving orders such as corporate executives, teachers, attorneys, doctors, etc., then the subtle permissive style of suggestion will probably be the most effective. Additional permissive style preference indicators to watch and listen for: Does he hesitate or ask "why?" frequently? Does he seem to deliberately assume a posture of relaxed self-control? Does he maintain his own, set expressions, making you feel like you're "working" to win him over? Are his reactions controlled, perhaps even skeptical? Does he seem to measure or question everything you say? These are all definite signs of a client who will benefit from your using the permissive approach.

In some instances, a permissive-style suggestion can use negative statements to get the desired results (NOTE: negative statements are *not* negative suggestions). By telling the subject what he does not have to do, you can often nudge him in the right direction. For example, *"You don't have to do anything you don't want to do. You don't have to make any kind of effort. You don't even have to bother trying to move about in the chair."* Here the permissive suggestion implies an idea just below the level of conscious awareness. Moving about in the chair is far more trouble than it's worth . . . an effort he must "bother trying" to make. As we discussed before, the word "try" implies failure, and the signal to the inner mind is, "it's too much trouble to move," so he doesn't.

THE THERAPEUTIC METAPHOR

Another type of suggestion is the use of the metaphor, or "therapeutic story", a technique often associated with the work of the late medical hypnotherapist, Milton Erickson, M.D. While Dr. Erickson was not the first to use this technique, he was undoubtedly its boldest and most influential proponent. Erickson frequently used analogies and metaphors within the framework of hypnosis to give his clients indirect suggestions outside of their conscious awareness. Sometimes he used lengthy and seemingly irrelevant dialogue to put his subject into hypnosis. Then he would tell stories or tales, much as you would to a child. However, the stories contained disguised suggestions of behavior that the subject would incorporate into his own, thus obtaining the therapeutic objective indirectly.

This type of suggestion is highly individual, and stories must be structured to fit the subject and the problem as closely as possible. It also requires a special skill that can be learned through practice.

The following therapeutic "story" was constructed by

Hoorwitz in his book, *HYPNOTIC METHODS IN NONHYPNOTIC THERAPIES.* Its purpose was to help a subject with obsessive behavior over which she felt like she had no control. She had indicated that the more she thought about the problem, the more obsessed she became with it, and the more she tried not to think about it, the more she thought about it. The therapist speaks as follows:

"This problem, of your thoughts about an urge versus your thoughts of controlling the urge, reminds me of a story I once heard about a dog who spent most of his time in the yard tied up to a post. This poor dog tried so hard to get away, and he pulled and he pulled, but the harder he pulled, the tighter the knot became which held him. Finally, after a great deal of pulling, the poor dog became thoroughly exhausted and simply gave up pulling, and he let go. And once he let go, the knot gradually loosened and finally the rope slipped from his neck, and he was free of the struggle."

DEEPENING SUGGESTIONS

Deepening suggestions are those specifically worded to actually deepen the existing hypnotic state. Almost anything can be used as a deepening suggestion, but some of the more common ones are as follows: "... **And now imagine that you are at the head of a stairway. As I count backwards from ten to one, imagine taking the steps down, and as you take each step, feel your body become more and more relaxed, feel yourself going deeper and deeper."**

ADDITIONAL EXAMPLES OF DEEPENING SUGGESTIONS

"... **With each breath you will go deeper and deeper",**

or "... **each time you open and close your eyes, you will go a thousand times deeper"**, or "... **as your arm comes slowly down to your lap, you will find yourself becoming more relaxed, and as your arm touches your lap, you will go even deeper than before."**

Almost anything can be used as a deepening suggestion. You may even use outside noises or other annoyances that might otherwise be a distraction:

"... **Each time you hear the traffic noise outside the window, you will go deeper and deeper"** or **"The sound of the telephone ringing only reminds you how very relaxed you are as you go deeper and deeper".**

IMAGERY SUGGESTIONS

Imagery suggestions are used along with other suggestions to create vivid mental pictures and set believable scenes. The subconscious mind loves imagery! For example, instead of simply saying, "I am going to count backwards from ten to one, etc. ...", it is much more desirable to paint a word picture of a beautiful carpeted staircase with ten steps to descend. The descriptions you use will help to provide believable images that are drawn from the subject's recollections of similar images from his own memory. Instead of just "clouds in the sky", speak of *"puffy, white pillows of clouds billowing in the endless blue sky"*. Instead of just "sunset at the beach", say *"the brilliant hues of orange, yellow, pink and purple blaze across the horizon and reflect their beauty in the vast mirror of the resting ocean."* You can be equally descriptive of emotions, speaking of **"pride welling up inside you as you look at your slim, trim and healthy new body, knowing that you have accomplished something significant, important for yourself".**

Or another:

"You are able to concentrate to such a degree that you will absorb the material before you like a sponge taking up water, retaining the most minute detail to recall whenever you need it".

Imagery suggestions can be intensified by using words that incorporate the senses whenever possible. Use what you know about human learning channels (see Chapter Five) and your client's own main representational learning system. Select verbs and word pictures that will elicit the most desirable response.

Here are examples of three different approaches to a guided relaxation image using a country scene as the setting:

For a primarily *visual* person, "... **imagine a beautiful, lush green countryside covered with white and yellow wildflowers, etc**..."

If the subject is primarily *auditory*, "... **listen to the sounds of the countryside—birds chirping, leaves rustling in the breeze, the splashing creek as it tumbles over the stones in its bed, etc**..."

For a primarily *kinesthetic* emphasis, "... **you can feel a gentle breeze blowing in the crisp country air—the warmth of the sun feels good on your shoulders, etc** ..."

POSTHYPNOTIC SUGGESTIONS

Posthypnotic suggestions are given during the hypnosis session to be carried out afterwards. The posthypnotic suggestion is heard and incorporated into the subconscious during hypnosis, but it is responded to—acted upon—on a subconscious level at a later time.

Accepting suggestions involves a personal belief system. Therefore, allow me to repeat that directives to the subconscious must be *realistic* and *thoroughly understandable*.

Only then will posthypnotic activity replace unwanted behavior. Posthypnotic suggestions must be keyed to the real needs and desires of the subject so that his emotional drive will be activated. His emotions must be involved if the suggestion is to be accepted. With proper motivation, a posthypnotic suggestion may last days or even years. Here are a few examples:

"When I awaken you at the numeral five, you will feel happy and alert, full of energy and enthusiasm."

"When you walk into the classroom tomorrow, you will find that you are actually looking forward to the exam, full of confidence and assurance that you'll do well because you are well-prepared."

"At mealtimes, you will discover that you are enjoying small portions of healthy food, and that you eat just enough to satisfy your body's needs."

"You will be pleased to notice that at the end of the day, you have not smoked a single cigarette. You simply did not think about cigarettes, did not want even one. You look forward to each and every day to come, knowing that you are now a non-smoker."

The fact is that anyone with whom we can communicate can experience the state of hypnosis if we take the time to understand the type and level of their natural suggestibility, and present them with suggestions which are properly designed to be acceptable to them. This profession offers us the unique opportunity to make a real difference in the lives of those who come to us for help.

CHAPTER EIGHT

CLINICAL HYPNOTHERAPY AS A PROFESSION

When I opened my first hypnotherapy practice in Rhode Island over 20 years ago, there were not very many other therapists in the country. When I moved to Orange County, California in the late 1970's, there still were not very many of us. My own private practice had reached a point where I needed help . . . There were far more people wanting my services than I could physically handle in a 6-day week.

It did not take me long to find out just how serious the therapist shortage was. There were not many other therapists available, and the few I interviewed had not had adequate training. As the need for a hypnotherapy education center became increasingly clear, I decided to start a school myself, a decision that would cause the focus of my professional efforts to shift from therapy to education.

Do I miss my private practice? Of course I do. There's nothing quite like hearing, "Dr. Krasner, you changed my life. Getting that weight off has made me a new woman!" or "I'm here because Jane Doe was so thrilled at the way you helped her to quit smoking. I think it's time for me to do the same thing." or "It's a miracle. I'm in control of my life, and my headaches have just disappeared."

On the other hand, teaching others to be effective hypnotherapists has its own rewards. Now, instead of hearing directly from the client, I hear from the new therapist. "It feels so good to be a part of this profession. Thank you for teaching me these invaluable skills," or, "Hypnotherapy has added a new dimension to my medical practice," or, "My own life has changed since I became a hypnotherapist. I have never known such emotional rewards. Thank you so much!"

I am very proud of my graduates and their successes, because in a way I feel that their successes are mine, too. If you are considering hypnotherapy as a profession, you have chosen a field that can provide personal pride and professional respect. It can also provide handsome financial rewards.

I caution you, however, to examine your incentives for choosing to be a hypnotherapist. If you have a strong desire to help others—if that is your guiding force—you will succeed. If your choice is based on other motives such as money or power, I encourage you to seek another direction. Your clients will know immediately whether you are sincere or not. They will also know if you really care about them, and they will respond accordingly.

THE POWER OF SUGGESTION AT WORK

People often change their attitudes and behavior when told to do so by someone who they perceive as holding a position of respect and prestige. We learned earlier that such a change is actually the person's acceptance of a *prestige suggestion.*

The power of the *prestige suggestion* is at work from the moment a client comes to you. The therapist-client relationship inherently contains a prestige suggestion: the therapist can help the client. The fact that the client has chosen to come to you for help establishes that.

The client's acceptance of this "pre-existing" suggestion often establishes the groundwork for effective therapy. Begin building on this suggestion immediately by demonstrating your competence and sincerity.

THE CONFIDENCE FACTOR

Although things such as your office, its furnishings, diplomas and awards, your personal appearance, etc., help define your overall external image as a therapist, the most significant factor in determining your—and your client's—success is your ability to convey sincerity, sensitivity, competence, and most of all, confidence.

Your client must sense that: 1) you believe in the therapy you are offering, 2) you believe that it can help him and 3) you believe that you can hypnotize him. If you do not believe in what you are doing, or if you have the slightest doubt that you can do it, you will instill that doubt in your client. Hypnosis clients are especially sensitive at picking up the covert attitudes and beliefs of their therapists.

THE CLINICAL SETTING

You may have a clinical hypnotherapy practice in an office, a clinic or your home. You may even choose to go where your clients are. I strongly recommend that you have your own office if at all possible because it is simply more professional. Regardless of the location, you must eliminate outside interferences as much as possible in order to create an atmosphere of calm and relaxation. Soft colors and comfortable surroundings are very important. A warm, welcoming environment that has a professional "look" is, itself a suggestion that "you can feel relaxed in this place." Lighting should be subdued, never completely dark. Make sure the subject's chair is comfortable. The back should be well-supported, and a headrest is helpful, though not required. I prefer to have my client seated in a plush recliner, close enough to my own chair that we can speak to each other easily. Ask your client to loosen tight collars and remove anything like jewelry, watches or glasses that might pinch the skin. Once he is seated, ask him to make himself comfortable with his feet flat on the floor (or uncrossed if you have a recliner) and his arms resting at his side. Make sure the position he is in is conducive to the relaxation of the entire body.

Remember that how one person looks and acts can greatly influence another person. Keep your appearance professional. Avoid looking casual and "laid-back" if you expect to be taken seriously.

Please think back now upon all of the material we have covered in this book. You know about suggestibility and your conscious/subconscious minds. You have demonstrated the mind-body effect for yourself. You learned about the brain and how information is processed.

THE CLINICAL INTERVIEW

Everything you have learned so far brings you to the most critical part of the hypnotherapy session: the pre-induction interview, or pre-talk. I have developed a very specific format which I have used for thousands of subjects. I teach that format in my classes, and in the next chapter I will give you a verbatim script of it for your own use.

The purpose of the pre-talk is four-fold:

1. to eliminate the fears and misconceptions the client may have about hypnosis;
2. to establish the therapeutic objective of the visit and enable you to determine the client's learning system;

3. to learn the client's motivation so that you can formulate effective suggestions;
4. to prepare the client for the induction through suggestibility tests.

It is also during this period that you further establish yourself with your client as an expert hypnotherapist. If your client believes that you can help him achieve his goals, in all likelihood you can. He will succeed if he expects to. Therefore, you must be at your professional best, maintaining control during the interview while showing your sincere desire to help him.

ELIMINATE FEARS

Most of the people who come to you will actually know very little about hypnosis. The scant knowledge they do have will most likely be based on pre-conceived ideas they have from reading fiction or watching stage shows. It is your responsibility to address these issues directly so that needless fears are alleviated.

Talk about stage shows and the expectancy of both the person volunteering and the audience. Tell your client how hypnosis does not mean loss of control. Let him know what hypnosis "feels like". Tell him as many times as you possibly can that he will hear and remember everything that is said during the entire session. It is up to you to explain what hypnosis really is and convince him of the benefits.

This is not the time to get into a protracted discussion about hypnosis that could literally go on for hours. I refer you again to the pre-talk script in the next chapter, especially for beginning therapists. I know it is effective.

ESTABLISH THE THERAPEUTIC OBJECTIVE

It is during this portion of the pre-talk that you will find out about the client's expectations and desires and what specific outcome he wants from the therapy. Beware of statements like, "My husband wants me to lose weight," or "My girlfriend said that I had to quit smoking," or "I'll have more friends if I make better grades." Statements like that should alert you that this client may not be ready to accept responsibility for his own problems, and he wants the outcome for someone other than himself. He must understand that he will be successful only if HE wants the outcome, and that unless he allows it to happen, it simply will not. He always has a choice, and only he can make it. If, on the other hand, he *believes* he can change and *expects* to change, his success is assured.

LISTEN FOR SUGGESTIONS

After your client has told you what he wants to accomplish (stop smoking, lose weight, reduce stress, etc.), you need to listen carefully for his motivation. What is the incentive for his wanting to make the change? The information you gather here is what you will use for the therapeutic suggestions you give him in hypnosis, so take careful notes as he speaks.

Note the following examples:

> Therapist: "How would your life change if you lost weight?"
>
> Client: "I would be able to wear swimsuits and look great when I go to the beach."

After hypnosis has been induced and you are ready to give therapeutic suggestions, an effective suggestion for this client would be, **"See yourself the size and shape you want to be. You are at the beach and enjoying all the admiring glances as you walk along the sand in your new swimsuit, etc."**

or

> Therapist: "When do you feel the most stress?"
> Client: "At work. Every time my supervisor Anne comes by my desk, she deliberately antagonizes me with one of her 'looks', and it makes me tense."

For this client, the therapeutic suggestion might be, **"See yourself at your desk at work. You are relaxed and busy, confident in your abilities to control your own life. See Anne as she approaches your desk. You look up and smile which makes you feel very good. You have a job to do, though, and you immediately return to your work as before, confident and relaxed, etc."**

During this time you also need to pay attention to the words your client uses and his body language. These are the cues that will tell you what his primary learning channel is, and what type of induction will be best for him. For example, if you are using a progressive relaxation induction, you can depict the same scene many different ways. It is up to you to choose the most effective way for this particular client. You may recall the examples in Chapter Seven of a relaxation scene using a country setting. Let us use a scene at the beach this time.

For a *kinesthetic*: **"As you walk along the beach, you feel the coarseness of the sand beneath your feet, the warmth of the sun spreading across your shoulders and back, etc."**

For an *auditory*: **"You are relaxing at the beach as you listen to the surf pounding, children laughing in the distance and the sound of the seagulls as they fly overhead, etc."**

For a *visual*: **"See yourself at the beach. The dazzling sand, the blue-green water stretching out as far as the eye can see under the clear bright blue sky, etc."**

Remember the imagination has power. The images you provide can predict a real outcome. When your client vividly imagines himself reaching his goals or improving his life, he actually activates certain brain activities that will cause those changes to happen. Just listen carefully to him. Your client inherently has all the answers. He will tell you all you need to know to help him.

USING SUGGESTIBILITY TESTS

When you have reached this stage of the pre-talk, your client has had a thorough explanation of what hypnosis is, and he has indicated his desire to move forward with the therapy.

The purpose of the suggestibility tests is to provide the client with a "right now" demonstration of hypnosis and how it feels. It allows you, the therapist, to determine to what degree the client will accept the suggestions offered. Tell the client what you are going to do. Be sure to say suggestibility "tests" because there is an automatic thought response of "pass/fail" when we think of tests. The client, wanting to "pass" the tests, will most likely be very cooperative and respond very nicely. For the exact wording that I teach, I refer you again to the next chapter where that is provided along with directions for giving the "tests".

SUGGESTIBILITY TESTS YOU CAN USE

There are many different suggestibility tests. My personal favorites are the postural sway test, the semaphore test and a variation on the hand-clasp test. Those are described step-by-step in the next chapter. Other wide-used tests are described below.

THE HAND CLASP TEST

Ask your client to stretch out his arms in front of him, clasp his hands gently together, lightly interlocking his fingers. Show him what you want him to do by briefly clasping your own hands together. Then say, **"Clasp your hands together and gaze at your knuckles. Now listen to me. I want you to picture your hands as gripping together like they are glued tightly. Lock your hands tightly together now . . . tighter and tighter, so tightly that you cannot pull them apart. Imagine now that they are glued so tightly together that you simply cannot part them, no matter how hard you try to pull them apart. When I count to 3, I want you to try to pull them apart, but you can't, they are stuck . . . 1,2,3 . . . try, but you cannot . . . When I touch them, they come apart easily and naturally. See?**

Give the suggestions in rapid succession as the client tries to meet the challenge. Do not keep him in the "stuck" position any longer than it takes for him to observe the phenomenon.

As soon as you have "released" his hands, compliment and tell him what an excellent subject he will be.

THE BACKWARD SWAY POSTURAL TEST

Ask your subject to stand in a relaxed position with his heels and toes together, hands at his sides. Stand about one foot behind him, and ask him to gaze upward in front of him at a spot on the wall. As he follows your directions, you say, **"That's right. Very good. Now look up at that spot and listen to my voice. Now as I place my hands beside your face and begin to draw them back, you will feel yourself falling back; you will fall back and I will catch you."** Begin pulling your hands back. You may flutter your fingers at the sides of the head where they can be seen out of the corner of the eyes. **"Continue falling back, falling, falling, falling back . . . back . . . that's good . . ."** As the subject falls backward, catch him by the shoulders and say something like, **"Excellent! You see, you concentrate so well that you will be a fine hypnotic subject!"**

THE EYEBALL TEST

Ask your client to keep his eyelids closed, to roll up his eyeballs, and to look upward at a point at the middle of his forehead. As he closes his eyes, begin the verbal instructions, lightly touching a spot high in the center of his forehead. Say, **"Keep your eyes closed. Your eyelids are sticking tightly together now . . . keep your eyeballs looking upward . . . up . . . up . . . Your eyelids are glued tightly together. They are stuck fast. The muscles of your eyes just cannot move . . . No matter how hard you try, they just will not open. Now try to open them. You cannot! Stop trying now, and just relax.**

From this moment, you will be able to open your eyes easily whenever you choose." Again, you must compliment your client when he follows your directions.

This particular test is actually based upon physiological facts rather than psychological ones. It is extremely difficult, if not impossible, to open the eyelids when the eyeballs are rolled up into the head. Naturally the eyeballs must come down before the eyelids can be opened. Therefore, if the client follows your instructions exactly, he will succeed at this "test".

THE HAND-DROP TEST

This test is an excellent method of choosing likely subjects from a group. Give the following instructions: **"All of you please put your arms in front of you. Now, close your eyes and visualize that you have a 10-pound bag of flour on the back of the palm of your right hand. Now, you can feel it getting very, very heavy. It is so heavy that your right hand is beginning to fall, beginning to get heavier and heavier as the heavy bag of flour is getting heavier and heavier, very, very heavy. Your right arm is getting very, very tired because it is so difficult to support this heavy weight."** (Look for good subjects among those participants whose right hand is well below the left.) **"Now, open your eyes, and observe your hands."**

THE OLFACTORY TEST

This test is also a good one for choosing subjects from an audience or group. You will need a capped bottle, preferably a perfume bottle, full of colored water. Hold the bottle up so that everyone can see it, and, as you take the stopper out or remove the cap, say, **"The smell of this perfume is drifting**

toward the back of the room. It is getting stronger and stronger, more and more pronounced. Will those of you who can smell this perfume please raise your hands?" Obviously, those who do smell the perfume are likely to be good hypnotic subjects.

THE RESISTANT CLIENT

What about the client who doesn't "pass" the tests?

What if, when asked to close his eyes, he does so briefly and opens them and looks at you? Or if you've told him his hands are stuck together, and he easily pulls them apart? While this does not happen very often, you must be prepared in case it does.

Always maintain your calm, controlled demeanor. Compliment the client, saying, **"Very good. You chose to open your eyes, part your hands, etc.. This indicates that you are always in control, free to accept or reject any suggestion you are given. This proves very well what we discussed before, doesn't it?"**

He will agree with you, of course. At that point you should also say something to this effect: **"However, we know that you really want to stop smoking (or lose weight, control your temper, etc.), or you would not be here, would you? If you really wish to be hypnotized at your own pace and by your own effort, all you have to do is to follow the ABC suggestions. If you follow these in sequence, you will readily develop a nice pleasant state of relaxation, provided that you really want to reach your ultimate goal. You do, don't you?"**

WORDING IS VERY IMPORTANT HERE. YOU MUST FORMULATE YOUR QUESTIONS ONLY IN WAYS THAT THE CLIENT CAN ANSWER "YES." This is not a time for discussion of things you have already covered. Your maintaining control at this point is essential to your client's success.

After he has agreed with you, ask him once again to close his eyes. (This technique is from the master teacher Dave Elman). Say, **"Now take a long deep breath and close your eyes. Now your eyelids are closed down. I want you to relax every tiny muscle and nerve in and around your eyelids. I want you to relax them so much that they wouldn't work if you wanted them to. Now test them; you'll see that you've been completely successful."** (Pause 3 seconds) **"All right, that's fine. Now stop trying and just relax. You'll find that at the count of three, they will open easily and naturally. One, two, three. Very good!"**

If, on the outside chance, he *does* open his eyes, you simply say, **"No, I told you to try only when you were sure they would not open ... Now close them again, and when you know they will not open, try to open them."** Obviously this presents a "Catch-22" for the client, but that's all right. You want him to be successful, and accepting these early suggestions is important to his success.

Never tell the subject that he is difficult to induce. Instead, use positive conditioning statements such as **"You did very well considering that it was the first time; you will do better and better each time."** Such positive statements set the stage for success in subsequent procedures.

THE INDUCTION

After you have completed the interview and conducted the suggestibility tests, your client should be confident and ready to begin the process. Make sure he is in a comfortable position. Encourage him to stretch out or lean back (whatever is appropriate for your furnishings), and proceed with the relaxation induction. You will find scripts for various relaxation inductions in the next chapter, in Chapter Ten and in the

Appendix.

THE HYPNOTIC VOICE

What about your voice? Is there even such a thing as a "hypnotic" voice? The truth about this probably lies somewhere between the watch-swinging carnival character and the "please sit back and relax," of today. Certainly, the voice as the transmitting medium is very important. During any eye-closed procedure, the client is focused entirely on the hypnotist's voice with no nonverbal clues for clarification ... But is there a certain correct "sound"? I don't think so. I have heard effective hypnotists' voices of both sexes: I would describe them variously as regular, soothing, deep, soft and/or reassuring.

Undoubtedly the most important factor the therapist's voice must convey is confidence ... confidence in himself and confidence that he can help his client. The therapist who is hesitant and administers suggestions in a weak or vacillating voice will transmit uncertainty which obviously will impede the success of the therapy.

The therapist's words during a hypnosis induction are often referred to as hypnotic "patter". The reason it is called a patter is because of the manner in which the words are spoken. The falling rain, the steady hum of a motor, the drip of a leaky faucet or any similar thing that goes on continuously in a monotonous way, effectively making us sleepy or drowsy, can be construed as a patter. Those sounds can actually hypnotize a person by repetition, causing him to inhibit his senses and awareness.

The words of the therapist should do the same thing. They should cause the senses to respond to the suggestions being given for relaxation and drowsiness. The words are spoken in such a way that the conscious mind is soothed into stilling its active thoughts and accepting the suggestions being given to rest and relax.

When considering how you should most effectively deliver the words, first consider the purpose of the words. If you are using a progressive relaxation, for instance, you might find that if you slightly distort particular words, you can achieve a special, enhanced effect. **"Feel your muscles becoming *soooo* relaxed, *loooose* and limp as you go deeper, *deeeeper* and even *deeeeper.*"**

I encourage you to practice your hypnotic "patter".

Use a tape recorder to record and listen to your own voice. In practicing, keep two things in mind:

(1) The client must hear what you say in order to respond—be sure you don't trail off into an inaudible whisper;

(2) Don't rush the process. Concentrate on being clear and rhythmic. When you become more familiar with inductions and therapy, you will find it easy to add inflections and dramatic pauses. If you do so without adequate practice, you run the risk of appearing incompetent. It isn't worth it.

Do use inflections when using words like "heavy" or "deep". These words sound ridiculous if you say them in a sing-song or lilted voice. Conversely, when you say "up, up, up" or "bright and alert" you don't want to sound like a dirge. Common sense will tell you when to slightly alter the pitch of your voice.

DEEPENING THE HYPNOTIC STATE

Like many other aspects of hypnosis, depth is a controversial matter among clinicians. There are many well-known hypnotic "depth scales" which have been scientifically developed by excellent hypnotherapists to determine hypnotic depth levels. So that you can become acquainted with these scales, I have reprinted some of them in the Appendix. However, in my opinion, the depth of hypnosis for motivational habit control and stress management is far less important to the success of the therapy than the personal motivation of the subject, and the therapist's correctly worded suggestions.

I would like to explain here the difference between light and deep hypnosis, and how you can recognize each state. When the subject is physically relaxed, light hypnosis is produced. When the subject is both mentally and physically relaxed, the hypnotic state is deep. After the progressive relaxation, the subject is likely to be physically relaxed, a state that I generally consider to be light hypnosis. The deepening suggestions are necessary to further relax him, to achieve mental as well as physical relaxation. This total relaxation of body and mind produces a state that is highly suggestible and likely to be very receptive to the therapeutic suggestions that come later.

Look for the following signs:

1. Flaccid facial muscles (sometimes called hypnotic "mask"),
2. Change of respiration to deep, relaxed breathing,
3. Fluttering of eyelids,
4. A listless, completely relaxed look.

Note: A very small percentage of people spontaneously go into deep hypnosis without ever going through the light state. They immediately become limp and very highly suggestible. These individuals, called somnambulists, do not need deepening suggestions. Deepening suggestions for these few people will produce a state so deep that they are difficult to work with. The inductions and suggestions in this book are those that you will use with the vast majority of your clients, those who do not become somnambulistic. For the somnambulist, a rapid induction is all that is necessary to prepare them for the therapy (See Chapter Ten).

ABREACTIONS

"Abreaction" is defined as the release of emotionally charged material from the subconscious. On rare occasions, you may have a client who begins to cry, or exhibit other strong emotional reactions in hypnosis. There are many therapists who believe that the best way to handle emotional trauma in hypnosis is to follow it through to its cause. I am not one of them. I firmly believe that in pursuing an emotional trauma, a hypnotherapist could easily find himself in the position of facing a situation that he is neither trained for nor qualified to handle.

Therefore, if while in hypnosis your client begins to display such behavior, I recommend the following verbiage: **"I want you to leave the place where you are now. Proceed to a place where you are happy and at rest . . . your subconscious mind will easily take you to this special place where you are relaxed and calm . . . so peaceful now . . . just relaxing and feeling wonderful"** . . . (pause for 5 seconds) . . . At this point your client will be calmed down and relaxed again. Ask him, **"Where are you now?"** (He will be able to answer your questions and remain in hypnosis.) After he describes to you where he is, you say, **"Very good . . ., and now as you continue to relax, you just stay calm and go deeper and deeper, calm and comfortable in every way."**

After a few more relaxation suggestions, I recommend that you bring the client out of hypnosis. In my opinion, it is not appropriate to give any therapeutic suggestions until you have spoken further with this client. After he has been awakened with more positive suggestions, discuss what happened with him. Only then can you determine whether you should continue with his therapy or if you should refer him to another professional for psychological or medical care.

THERAPEUTIC DISCRIMINATION

The type of hypnotherapy I practice and teach is to be used to help overcome motivational habits ... to modify behavior patterns in order to bring about the desired change. This encompasses literally hundreds of possibilities that include many different behaviors and almost limitless possibilities for changing them.

However, there are specific problem areas for which hypnosis is not well-suited, and there are certain types of problems which you should avoid treating unless you are a qualified medical or psychology professional. Any time you are in doubt about the acceptability of any therapeutic situation, I urge you to make whatever referrals are appropriate. Give him the names of at least two professionals, so he can make his own decision about whom he consults. Do not hesitate to do this, not only for your client's sake, but also for the sake of your own professional reputation. In the litigious world of today, you must handle these cases with professional discretion and care in order to avoid the possibility of trouble later. You can build a practice with more clients than you can handle if you recognize your own areas of expertise and refer the others to other professionals. Just remember the phrase I teach in my classes: *If in doubt, refer it out.*

THERAPEUTIC SITUATIONS TO AVOID

When it comes to deciding whether or not you should proceed with a particular client, you will have to exercise your own good judgment. In truth, the vast majority of people who will seek your services are those whom you can treat very effectively.

However, as a general rule, there are four types of problems that you should consider candidates for referral: clients who are obviously psychotic, those who have unrealistic expectations, those who have borderline personalities or those who want you to deal with a medical problem. All of these individuals may be helped with hypnotherapy, but only in the hands of a highly qualified, widely experienced professional who uses it in adjunct with another type of therapy.

The *psychotic personality* will likely come to you exhibiting intense outbursts of emotion, such as uncontrolled crying or screaming. They may suffer from hallucinations, rage, unfounded fears or amnesia. Hypnosis cannot create a psychosis where none existed before, but a hypnotic state can temporarily intensify an existing condition.

The person with *unrealistic expectations* is one who thinks hypnosis in and of itself can cure anything and whose motivation comes from an outside source. I discussed this earlier in this chapter when I mentioned individuals who are seeking treatment because someone else wanted them to. Another person in the category of "unrealistic expectations" is the one who is seeking something which is obviously impossible. For instance, if a man comes to you and wants to make some change in himself so his girlfriend will love him more, you would have to tell him that although you could help him in the way he deals with his girlfriend, you can do nothing about her feelings toward him!

You will recognize what I call a *borderline personality* when you hear descriptions of bouts with depression and feelings of profound hopelessness. The people who suffer from such consuming, heavy anxiety may have a host of psychological problems that even they are not aware of. Again, your client is better served by your professional referral.

It is generally easy to tell when a *medical referral* is in order. This is most often the client who comes to you with complaints of chronic or intractable pain. If the complaint is a headache, for instance, you must not assume that it is stress-induced. Yes, you could relieve the client of the pain, but that would not remove an existing medical condition such as a brain tumor. NEVER take a client's word for such a thing. To protect him and yourself, you must either have a written medical referral or refer the client to a physician.

CHAPTER NINE

THE KRASNER METHOD OF CLINICAL HYPNOTHERAPY

In the previous chapter, Clinical Hypnotherapy as a Profession, I presented a general guide for professional hypnosis practitioners. I will be the first to admit that there is nothing sacred about any single method of hypnosis. Getting where you want to go is much more important than how you get there.

However, in this chapter I want to share with you the therapeutic techniques that I developed during my many years of private practice. My clients were successful, and they referred their friends to me. There is no finer testimony to the success of a therapist than that.

As you practice and grow more comfortable in your role as a therapist, you will probably develop your own "method." For now, though, I recommend your using mine . . . it works.

THE PRE-INDUCTION INTERVIEW

For me, the pre-induction interview is the *most important* part of the entire hypnotic process. If you handle the pre-induction interview correctly, the rest will fall easily into place.

You are the therapist. The person in front of you is your client. He wants to make a change in his life, and he has come to you for help.

After the initial introductions and brief discussion of the client's reason for wanting hypnotherapy (see previous chapter), you (the therapist) must take and keep immediate control. Now, I do not mean "know-it-all" or arrogant control. I mean a confident, self-assured direction of the session that will give your client a feeling of positive expectancy.

This is such an important topic that I am going to first go over it section by section, explaining each step as we go. You may use the therapist's dialogue verbatim, or adapt it to your own style. Do not leave any of it out, though, because as you will see, there is a reason for every single step. Assume now that the amenities are concluded. You (the therapist) take control of the session by saying:

THE PRE-TALK DIALOGUE	COMMENTS
1. **"Let *me* tell *you* about hypnosis."**	This establishes you (the therapist) as the authority (remember prestige suggestions?—this is one)
2. **"You will not feel hypnotized, nor will you be out of control.** **"You've seen hypnosis shows, haven't you?"** (Client answers yes.) **"It looks like the subject's mind is being controlled, doesn't it?"** (Client answers yes.)	At this point you must remove the three most common misconceptions that you are likely to encounter. Notice the wording. Frame the question to elicit the answer you want.

3. **"These people volunteered, didn't they?** (Client answers yes.) **Weren't they volunteering to have fun?** (Client answers yes.) **The truth is, on stage they will accept the hypnotist's suggestions as long as they have no moral objection. However, the same man who on stage will accept the suggestions to forget his name . . . the same one who will happily entertain the audience by waddling around quacking like a duck . . . will certainly not accept a suggestion to rob a bank or hurt anyone . . . His critical sensor will take over immediately, say, "No way!", and he will either simply refuse to comply, or he will spontaneously come out of hypnosis."**

You keep getting affirmative answers. Every time that happens, you gain new confidence from the client, and make "yes" answers more likely. Here the client may begin to realize that it is the person on stage who is *really* in control, not the hypnotist.

4. **"You know, the funny thing is that those people on stage, when asked, "Were you hypnotized?" will invariably say "No." When asked "How do you know?" they will say *every time*— "I heard every word that was said." Further, if asked,**

You are "setting up" for the client's own hypnotic experience expectations

"Why, then, did you behave like that?" they will say, again, every time, "I don't know!" They obviously expected to go into a deep trance or sleep which of course simply doesn't happen."

5. **"Let me demonstrate to you what hypnosis really feels like. Close your eyes, please. That's it.** (pause 5 seconds) **It just feels like that! You will remain aware of everything at all times."**

You want them to know that there will be no "weird" feeling, no loss of consciousness or hearing.

6. **"Now keep your eyes closed and place your hands in your lap."** (client complies) **"Now put your feet together."** (client complies)

Here they easily experience following your suggestions.

7. **"Now go into the corner, please, and stand on your head."** (client opens eyes and objects)

This reinforces the control issue. The client will relate his own experience here to the experience of the person hypnotized on stage that was discussed earlier.

8. **"You agreed to close your eyes, to put your hands in your lap and to put your feet together. However, you weren't about to stand on**

I believe it is very important to let the client know that *he* is responsible for his own motivation and participation.

your head. My point is this: Hypnosis simply cannot *make* you do anything. It only makes it easy to achieve what you want to achieve. It cannot make you *want* to do it, either. That's *your* part."

9. **"The body is only a robot, controlled by the mind. What the mind sees, the body tends to do. Think of a lemon.** (Go through the imagery on page 30) **What happened?"** (The client will tell you he salivated, or had a sour taste, etc.) **Now think of something frightening.** (Pause) **What happened this time?** (Client will tell you that his heart began to beat faster, or that he felt anxious, etc.) **"Of course, there is nothing frightening here, but the body didn't know that. It just believed what it was told by your mind, just like it did with the lemon. Therefore, if it is told that it doesn't want cigarettes any more** (or too much food, or to react a certain way, etc.), **it won't, because it doesn't know that it ever did."**

Once the misconceptions are handled, it is important to get into the "body is a robot" theory. The lemon demonstration is excellent for this.

10. **"Do you have any questions?"**	At this point the client may be confused, but the concepts are beginning to come together. The client seldom has questions. If he does, answer them patiently and completely, but succinctly.
11. **"Tell me. How would your life improve if you . . .?"** (lost weight, stopped smoking, relaxed more, studied harder, etc.)	Listen very carefully to the answer to this question. *Your client will give you the words to use in his therapy session.* He is telling you what is important to him, and what his motivation is. Write down what he says.
12. **"Now I'd like to do a few suggestibility tests to see how you'll do in hypnosis. Is that all right with you?"** (client always agrees—after all, he has come to you for hypnosis)	The client is still unconvinced that *he* can be hypnotized—even though he may have cooperated completely. Always use the word *test.* This way, he thinks that if he "succeeds" in passing the tests, he will be a good subject.
13. **"Stand up here in front of me please, feet together, heels and toes even. That's it. Very good. Now I want you to watch my ring."** (I hold my hand above their head [ring turned inside] so that they must look up to see	This "test" is the beginning of the client's belief system being changed. The fact is, that when human beings stand with their heels and toes together and close their eyes, they must sway. However, the client doesn't

it. A ring is not necessary. You may just as well say, 'Watch my hand') **"As you watch my ring you will feel your eyes begin to close and you will begin to sway back and forth, back and forth. As I tap you on the shoulder, you feel your body falling forward, and you allow it to, knowing that I will catch you."** (client falls forward onto your hands.

know this. He thinks he is responding to suggestion, and his belief in hypnosis is increased. And with that, guess what else is increased? The probability of his success!

14. **"Good. You did very well on that one! Let's try another . . . Now hold both arms out in front of you about shoulder height. Now close your eyes and imagine that I have just placed a very heavy book—a dictionary—on this hand.** (Just lightly touch the hand) **At the same time I tie a string around this wrist,** (Lightly touch the underside of the wrist of the other hand) **to which is tied a big red helium balloon."** I proceed with the semaphore demonstration described on page 38.

Every time I can demonstrate to the client that his body responds to his imagination, the greater his own belief in the therapy becomes. (This exercise gives you a wonderful opportunity to use your own "voice") Make the word "heavy" sound heavy, and likewise "lighten" your tone in describing the balloon. Give the balloon a bright color. Remember the mind loves adjectives.

15. **"Now open your eyes and look at how one arm has gone up and the other has gone down. Isn't that interesting? There was no book and no balloon, yet your arms are apart!** (The client is always amazed and enjoys this.) **I told your robot that there was a book and a balloon there, and it believed me. Your mind *"saw"* them, and your body reacted accordingly. It will do the same thing when it is told that it is a non-smoker. Now I can show you hypnosis with your eyes wide open."**

Again, I take the opportunity to reinforce the concept that the "body is a robot", blindly following whatever instructions the mind gives it.

16. **"O.K. Now clasp your hands together with your fore-fingers separated. Imagine that there is a vise clamped around them, and as I tighten on the vise, your fingers get closer together. Watch them as I tighten this device and they move in tighter and tighter until they are completely together."** (I make a twisting motion with my hands on either side of their outstretched fingers, simulating a "tightening-up"

This is always a surprising demonstration for the client. As they successfully participate here, their belief in their own ability to be hypnotized is profoundly deepened.

motion. See illustration at right). **As his fingers touch each other, say "Now your fingers are stuck together, so tightly that you cannot get them apart, no matter how hard you try. The harder you try, the tighter they are stuck. Very good. But when I touch them, you see how easily they are to get apart."** (Lightly touch his fingers with your own. The fingers will come apart. Client often looks amazed and puzzled at this) **"Was there really a vise? Of course not. Again, your robot body obeyed the orders your mind gave it, just like it did with the book and balloon."**

Imaginary vise causes fingers to tighten.

Occasionally you will have a client who resists following these suggestions. He may look up at you and spread his fingers wide open, just the opposite of what you are telling him. Remember the discussion in the previous chapter on the resistant client. When this happens, you simply refer back to the numerous times he followed your suggestions and to your previous explanation of stage hypnosis. You say:

"See? Even though you *'saw'* the book and the balloon, and you *'saw'* the lemon, you chose not to accept the suggestion that

your fingers were in a vise and stuck together. You just demonstrated what I've told you all along. You are *always* in control. The choice is *always yours.* I feel sure that since you've come here to stop smoking (lose weight, control stress, etc.)**, you will choose to accept the suggestions to stop smoking, don't you agree?"** (The client will answer yes. After all, he has come to you for help.)

NOTE: Once the client has participated in the above tests, I may or may not show them the pendulum and/or pencil demonstrations (see Chapter Four), or do further suggestibility tests. If the client is cooperative and highly suggestible it is a good idea. He enjoys it, and it further strengthens his belief that the therapy will work. This is strictly a matter of personal choice. At this point the client is very easy to put into hypnosis. Why? Because his belief in his own ability to be hypnotized was strengthened when he "passed" the suggestibility tests; even if he did not cooperate with the vise test, his concerns about losing control are eliminated. Either way, your client will be a better subject.

Immediately after the last suggestibility test, you should proceed with the induction. There are a number of inductions that you may use, but I always prefer to use the progressive relaxation method when doing therapy. Without a doubt, this type of induction is the most dependable, especially for the relatively inexperienced hypnotherapist, and it affords the least likelihood of being misunderstood by the client. In fact, if the client actually follows the steps for the relaxation of the body, the conscious mind will also be relaxed. When that happens, of course, it is easily distracted from critical assessment, and hypnosis follows easily and naturally. Additionally, I find that the client feels cheated if I do a rapid induction. They love the relaxation and the feeling they have when they leave my office. Who *doesn't* enjoy a relaxing hour of attention? Give your clients the time they are paying for . . . and deserve.

I have a favorite progressive relaxation which I will share with you here. There are many other good ones, one of which you will find in Chapter Ten on page 138, and two more which you will find in the appendix. Now back to your client. You have him comfortably seated, and you begin:

Sit back, relax and just close your eyes. In a very few moments you're going to be more relaxed than you've ever known yourself to be. I'm going to mention certain parts of your body, and as I do, I want you to just feel that part begin to relax—just feel that part begin to relax. In order to help you relax, I want you to visualize yourself on a very beautiful little white sailboat. You feel the sun warming every muscle, nerve and bone in your body. The sky is the most beautiful blue you have ever seen—just a few white, puffy clouds lazing in the sky, and as you hear the sounds of the sea and the sounds of the sailboat, you begin to feel more and more relaxed. As I mention certain parts of your body, you'll feel that portion just begin to relax, so that in a few moments, you will be more relaxed than you've ever known . . . Starting with the forehead, I want you to feel all the little frown lines, all the little worry lines in the forehead, just seem to disappear. The forehead smooths out, feels so relaxed, and you feel this relaxation coming around the eyes. Now the eyelids seem to become very, very heavy, so heavy they don't seem to want to open. They may want to flutter a little bit, but that's OK . . . just feel how heavy they are . . . and as the relaxation comes down around the facial

muscles now, all the muscles in the facial area just begin to relax. Relaxation comes further down around the mouth now, and all the hundreds of little muscles around the mouth just start to relax...so much so that the lower jaw becomes heavy and the teeth part. Your mouth may even open up a little bit with relaxation as you continue deeper and deeper relaxed. Feel this relaxation now around your lower jaw, behind your ears so that all the little nerve endings behind the ears just seem to relax as you continue deeper and deeper, and even deeper as the sounds of the sea seem to say deeper, deeper, deeper. The relaxation goes to the back of the neck now, down around the shoulder, so much tension seems to go to our shoulders . . . but now you feel the shoulders just begin to relax. You can even feel them drop a bit. The relaxation goes to the backbone now, and as it goes down the spinal column, it seems to go out to the sides, so that every muscle, nerve and fiber in your back just seems to relax . . . The relaxation seems to come now to the small of your back, and around the curve of the back. This warm sense of relaxation comes to the back of the thigh now, and into the hollow of the knee, around the calf of the leg, around the heel, to the bottom of the foot. And each and every toe just relaxes even more as you go deeper, deeper, even deeper, hearing the sounds of the sea as the little boat gently rocks you deeper, and even deeper . . . Calm, very peaceful, relaxed, the whole head and back area seem very, very relaxed . . . Now we will proceed with the rest of you, starting with the throat muscles, feel your throat muscles just start to relax. The relaxation comes down the fronts of the shoulders, down the upper arm, over the elbow, down the forearm to the hand as each and every finger relaxes more and more as you go deeper and deeper, deeper, even deeper . . . Feel the relaxation coming back to the throat muscles, down into the chest, and all the muscles and organs within the chest area just begin to relax, continuing far into the stomach area, as all the

muscles and organs within the stomach area seem to relax . . . relaxation going down now into the thighs, over the knees, more and more as you continue to go deeper, deeper, and even deeper . . . Calm, peaceful, and very, very relaxed . . . I'm going to let you rest for a moment, but when you hear my voice again, you will continue to go even deeper and deeper, calm, peaceful and relaxed. Imagine yourself on that little white sailboat, gently swaying back and forth, drifting deeper and even deeper. . . *(Pause for a moment)*. . . **And just continuing to go deeper now, I want you to leave that little sailboat now, and see you and me standing at the head of a beautiful flight of ten stairs. These stairs are covered in your favorite color of carpet. We are going to go down these stairs now, as I count backwards from ten to zero, each numeral will take you deeper, deeper, and even deeper. Are you ready to go down these stairs with me now? Nod your head for me, please.** *(Pause, and wait for slight nod.)*. . . **Very well . . . Ten. Take that first step down . . Nine, deeper and deeper . . . Eight, way down now . . . Seven, deeper, even deeper, . . . Six, deeper, feeling very relaxed, . . . Five, deeper, deeper, . . . Four, deeper. Three, going deeper still, . . . Two, deeper and deeper, feeling very calm . . . One . . . At the next number, you will enter this beautiful place of peace and tranquility called deep, deep hypnosis . . . More relaxed, more peaceful than you've ever known yourself to be . . . Is that all right with you? Nod your head, please . . .** *(Pause, and watch for slight nod.)* . . . **Wonderful . . . ZERO.**

When you have completed the progressive relaxation, your client will be hypnotized. You will know it. But he won't! Don't forget, the client may be hypnotized, but the client *does not believe he is!*

SIGNS OF HYPNOSIS

In addition to the signs discussed in the previous chapter (flaccid facial muscles, change in respiration, fluttering eyelids and a listless look), look for a slight smile on his face. When you suggest heaviness in his arms or legs, watch him as he slightly strains against the invisible force that makes them so heavy. As your client visualizes and reacts to simple suggestions, you will know that he is in a responsible hypnotic state, ready to accept therapeutic suggestions. To be doubly sure, lift the client's arm about six inches by encircling your fingers around his wrist, using a very light touch, and let it go. The hypnotized person will allow the arm to "plop" into his lap with absolutely no resistance. (In the waking state the arm would have either stayed suspended, or the fall to the lap would be visibly controlled.)

Now your client is in the hypnotic state. He is definitely hypnotized. You know it. You are certain. You have done your pre-induction talk well, so the client *knows* that hypnotized people don't "feel" hypnotized. He knows that hypnotized people hear every word said around them. And he *knows* that hypnotized people never think they have been hypnotized. But guess what? When you bring him out of hypnosis he *will* say ... *"I wasn't hypnotized. I heard every word you said."* I do not care how well you have explained everything. I do not care how many times he agreed with you and indicated to you that he understood every word you said. Count on it. *He will say those words.* At that point you can do nothing but argue with him ... which is foolish, frustrating and an exercise in futility.

CONVINCERS

Therefore, *when you are certain that the client is hypnotized,* I recommend that you do some simple demonstrations with him that I call "convincers" because they are designed to do just that! They are for the single purpose of convincing the client, *after* the session, that he was indeed hypnotized. Incidentally, you do not want him convinced so that you can be right; you do it so that the therapy will work for *him*. Proceed with the "convincers" part as follows:

THERAPIST TO HYPNOTIZED CLIENT	NOTES
"As you continue to relax, I am going to count from one to three. At the count of three you'll find that you can't open your eyes, even if you try. You simply cannot open them. One, two, three. (Client tries to open eyes.) **That's fine. Don't even try anymore. You're doing so well now as you go deeper and deeper . . .**	On three, look for a slight muscular pull in the client's eyelids. As soon as you see the effort, continue.
. . . And as you go deeper, just concentrate on your left arm . . . Notice how heavy it is . . . so very heavy. In fact, it is so heavy that when you try to lift it, it won't go up . . . just too heavy. (Client tries to lift arm.) **That's okay. It's just too much work . . . don't even try anymore as you relax even more . . .**	Again, I look for the effort. This is easy to spot by watching the arm for muscular contractions. After the first effort, as before, continue.

. . . **And now I want you to imagine that there is a string tied around your right wrist and attached to the other end of that string is a large, bright-red, beautiful helium balloon, floating up, up, to the sky. As I count from one to three, your right arm will lift and go higher with that beautiful balloon. One, two, three.** (Client's arm lifts.) . . . **I am going to count from one to ten now, and when I reach the count of ten, you'll find that you can't put your arm down** . . . **when you try to put it down, it goes up instead** . . . **You are amused as you observe this happening** . . . **One, two, three, four, five, six, seven, eight, nine, ten** . . . **You try to put your arm down, but it goes up instead** . . . (Client tries to lower arm and arm goes higher) . . .

This entire sequence is one that is a good dramatic example for later reference. That is why you must ask the client to observe what is happening.

. . . When I ask you to put your arm down, you will find that it goes down easily . . . and as it goes down, you find that you relax even 100 times deeper . . . You may lower your arm now as you go even deeper into this wonderful, relaxed state . . .

Observation is the key here. You should be certain that every direction you suggest is followed.

Now, you can begin to give the actual therapeutic suggestions. These suggestions will vary from client to client, of course. In the last chapter on self-hypnosis, there are several "scripts" that you easily adapt to formulate the suggestions you will use for each client.

Do you remember when, in the pre-talk, you asked the client how his life would improve? Now is the time to use that vital information. This is his personal session; personalize it with names, places, events, etc. that he has given you . . . this is the key to his success.

For example, if he told you that he wants to stop smoking because he likes to run with his friends Dick and Jane, but he's too short-winded, you might say, **"See yourself running steadily and strongly, breathing deeply with ease. Imagine Dick and Jane running alongside of you, fully enjoying your running with them. Notice how proud you feel because you are a non-smoker . . . etc."**

Or, if he has told you that he wants to manage his stress at work your words might be, **"Imagine now that you are sitting at your desk. There are dozens of papers on it, but they are orderly and neat. You know that you can do only one thing at a time. You do your job efficiently and calmly. You respond to inquiries in a relaxed and confident manner, knowing that you are centered and in control, . . . etc."**

These personal suggestions are very important. The therapy

is much more meaningful when they contain the client's own personal reasons for wanting change, the reasons he gave you in the pre-talk interview. Also, this method serves to enormously increase the client's motivation because of his emotional involvement in the imagery.

After you have given the therapeutic suggestions, it is time for you to bring the client back to full waking consciousness. Increase the lilt and energy in your voice as you say:

"I'm going to wake you up now at the count of five. At five, you will open your eyes, bright and alert, full of energy, and feeling perfectly wonderful. One, coming up now. Two, more and more, three, more awake four, bright and alert five, wide awake now, feeling wonderful! How do you feel?"	Increase the tempo of your voice (not the volume) to sound cheerful and energetic.

At this point, the client will say something to this effect, "Fine, I was very relaxed."

Then, guess what he'll say? Yes, indeed. He will say, *"I don't think I was hypnotized, though. I heard every word you said!"*

Never argue with a client. If you have done the pre-talk correctly, *you don't have to.* Instead say,

THERAPIST	CLIENT
"Why wouldn't your eyes open when you tried to open them?"	*"I don't know."*

"And why wouldn't your arm come up when you tried to lift it?"	*"I don't know."*
"And what about your right arm? Why couldn't you put it down? Isn't it kind of unusual for you to go around with your arm in the air like that?"	*"I don't know. Maybe I was hypnotized after all."*

Can you understand now why I call these earlier demonstrations "convincers"? The client *must* believe he was hypnotized in order for the therapy to be successful.

Do not omit any of these steps. They are all there for a reason. If you follow the steps as instructed, you will be successful.

CHAPTER TEN

INDUCTION METHODS

Actually, there is no limit to the number of techniques that can be used to elicit the hypnotic response. In fact, I quite agree with Dave Elman who said, "There is no way in which you cannot hypnotize a person once you know how to utilize suggestion."

The fact is that the client (or the person being hypnotized) always enters the state of hypnosis in a natural way, of his own accord, simply by following the suggestions of the hypnotist. Therefore, any set of suggestions which the subject will accept and follow that results in the distraction of his conscious mind is an effective induction.

There are several kinds of inductions, varying in length of time involved, general approach and style. One hypnotherapist may find a particular technique more suitable than another. All hypnotherapists have their favorites. Whatever the induction method used, however, it must accomplish the following:

- relaxation of body
- distraction of conscious mind
- narrowed focus of attention
- increased sensory awareness

- reduced awareness of physical surroundings
- increased awareness of internal sensations

THE RELAXATION INDUCTION

As I stated in the previous chapter, I believe the progressive relaxation induction to be the most effective and "foolproof" way to induce hypnosis in a therapeutic setting. This is because it systematically relaxes every muscle in the body. I have had hundreds of students in my classes read a relaxation induction directly from a script and successfully put a classmate into hypnosis on their first try. My own favorite version of that type of induction is also included in that chapter. There are many versions of relaxation inductions. I will give you an example of another one here, and you will find additional versions in the Appendix.

RELAXATION INDUCTION II

Place your subject in a chair or on a sofa, and ask him to place his hands loosely on his lap or alongside his body. Ask him to relax his entire body by taking a deep breath in and letting it out very slowly. You speak as follows:

"Now I want you to take another deep breath and let it out very slowly . . . relaxing your entire body. Close your eyes, and listen to my voice . . . Start concentrating on an imaginary spot on the center of your forehead, and as you concentrate on that imaginary spot, relaxation will occur throughout your body . . . That relaxation will start with the muscles in the top of your scalp, working down over the forehead . . . down over your facial muscles, further down your neck muscles, over your chest, now over your waist . . . over your hips and thighs . . . Your entire body is becoming very relaxed. As you listen to the sounds of my voice, you

will begin to notice the weight of your body as your legs become very heavy and tired ... Your arms are becoming very heavy and tired ... Your neck, shoulders and head are also becoming heavy and tired, feeling loose and limp, heavy and relaxed. As I continue to talk to you now, the tones of my voice tend to lull into a very restful, peaceful, calm state of being ... Your mind is drifting through space as if it were floating on a cloud, so completely relaxed all over ... Your body is growing heavy and tired as you go down, down, deeper and deeper, all worldly things seem very remote now as you go down into the most restful sleep you have ever known ... A wonderful, warm, restful and peaceful sleep, a dreamless sleep ... Your eyes are closing even more tightly now, as they are heavier and heavier, and you feel so relaxed all over ... All muscular tension, all mental tension has disappeared now ... You can feel everything letting go, as you go deeper and even more relaxed ... From this moment on, every word I say to you will only carry you deeper and deeper to sleep until I give you the signal to awaken ... So deep now that only relaxation seems to matter."

FIXATION/FASCINATION INDUCTION

The fixation/fascination-type of induction requires that the subject's attention be directed to a very narrow point of interest such as the hypnotherapist's eyes, a swinging pendulum, a flickering flame, an hourglass or even a spot on the wall. All of the variations on this induction work on the basis of the same principles of misdirected attention and sensory fatigue. The subject directs his attention upon the suggested object so intently that he is too occupied to analyze what is happening, and because of the intensity of his staring at that object, ocular fatigue is created. This is probably the most widely used method of hypnosis. To use this induction, you ask your client to assume a comfortable position and to stare intently at whatever you have chosen as the focal point. The point should be slightly above his normal line of vision so that he has to look upward in order to see it. You say:

"Pick a spot on the ceiling (or wherever else you choose) **and gaze at it. Keep on looking at the spot and listen to my voice. Relax as you stare at the spot. Feel yourself relaxing all over . . . deeper and deeper. As you keep staring at the spot, your eyes will become very heavy and drowsy. Your entire body is becoming heavier and heavier . . . your arms, heavy . . . limp and relaxed . . . legs limp and heavy and relaxed . . . feet are becoming relaxed . . . relaxed all over. As you keep staring at the spot, your eyes may begin to tear, to blink . . . you are getting drowsy . . . heavy . . . sleepy . . . a wonderful feeling, warmth and relaxation flowing all through your body as you relax more deeply than ever before . . . your eyes blinking . . . tearing . . . they feel like closing . . . closing soon. When they close . . . the sound of my voice makes you sleepier and sleepier . . . you are going to fall into a pleasant state of relaxation . . . eyes will close soon . . . think of sleep . . . it is getting harder and harder . . . for you to focus your eyes . . . they are closing . . ."**

Once you have completed the external focus, tell the subject to: **"Keep on going deeper . . . as I count backward from 5 to 0, you will keep going deeper and deeper . . . asleep . . . listen to my voice as you let go and allow yourself to drift deeper and deeper. You will awaken only when I tell you to . . . .the sound of my voice makes you go deeper and even deeper . . . you love this feeling of complete relaxation, letting go all over, feeling wonderfully relaxed as you go deeper and deeper inside yourself . . ."**

or another version:

Place your hands on the subject's shoulders and look into his eyes. Point your index finger to your own eyes as you say:

"Look into my eyes and relax . . . you are going into deep

sleep ... deep sleep ... your eyes are closing now ... you are going deep asleep ... deep asleep ... your eyes are feeling so very heavy that you just don't want to keep them open any longer ... so heavy that they just want to close ... very good ... deep asleep ... and even deeper as you relax more and more ... your entire body feels loose and limp and calm ... you feel so comfortable and relaxed, and with each breath you take you continue to go deeper and deeper ... much deeper now as the sound of my voice takes you deeper still."

CONVERTING A TEST INTO HYPNOSIS INDUCTION

Some people are so highly suggestible that you will be able to achieve hypnosis almost instantaneously. Experience will help you recognize such easy subjects.

Converting a suggestibility test to hypnosis is feasible with a small percentage of your clients. You will be able to identify such a subject not only by his strong responses to testing, but also by his appearance of being slightly dazed and confused, perhaps speaking with a muted voice. If you recognize that you have such a client, and you want to go directly into the hypnosis, proceed as follows: After the Hand Clasp Test (See Suggestibility Tests, Chapter Eight, page 105), say:

"Now your hands are stuck tight ... tight together ... you cannot pull them apart ... try, but you cannot ... just stop trying and go deeply asleep, now, that's right, feeling so relaxed and comfortable in every way ... deep, calm, relaxed and peaceful. Now when I try to pull your hands apart, they will loosen and come apart easily, and as they do, you fall into an even deeper sleep ... relaxing even more and more, so comfortable and feeling so wonderful."

SPIRAL HYPNO-DISC INDUCTION

When using a hypno-disc as a fixation point, give the following suggestions for eye closure:

"Keep you eyes fastened on the center of the wheel ... as you watch it ... notice that it vibrates ... the white circles become more prominent, then the black circles become more prominent. The circles seem to fade into the distance and you begin to feel as if you are being drawn into the circle ... your breathing is deep and regular ... you are getting drowsy, very drowsy ... soon you will be deeply relaxed, going deeper and deeper with each and every breath you take ... As I count backward from 5 to 1, your eyes will close, and you will fall into a deep hypnotic sleep ... 5 ... 4 ... 3 ... 2 ... 1 ... deep asleep."

RAPID INDUCTIONS

The rapid induction produces the hypnotic state almost instantly. This induction, like the "test conversion" induction, is most successful with highly suggestible subjects. Be sure your client falls into this category before using a rapid induction method on him; some people find it too abrupt and not relaxing at all. This is the type of induction that is most closely associated with theatrics and stage hypnosis because it makes for rather dramatic demonstrations.

When you employ this method, give short, rapid commands such as the following:

"Now close your eyes. Lower your head until your chin is on your chest, and go deeply, deeply asleep. Good. Now, with each breath you take, you will go even deeper."

A variation on the rapid induction technique is as follows: With an air of complete confidence in yourself, raise the subject's arm, extend it straight out in front of him and say:

"As I raise your arm, it will become stiff and rigid ...

as stiff and rigid as a bar of steel, so rigid . . . you just cannot lower it . . . you cannot lower it no matter how hard you try . . . try . . . hard . . . you cannot lower it . . . it's just too much trouble, so stop trying . . . and now go deep asleep . . . deep asleep . . . now you can lower your arm, and as you do so, you take a deep breath and go even deeper . . . that's right . . . so deep that your entire body relaxes . . . deeper with every breath you take . . . very good . . . "

THE STAR METHOD INDUCTION

This induction, developed by Dr. Bernard Gindes, relies completely on your subject's ability to visualize. Have your subject comfortably seated in a chair, and ask him to close his eyes. Say:

"I want you to imagine a star. The star is suspended far above you in the distance. Now just imagine that star, concentrating all of your attention on it. Now the star is moving forward, moving forward, closer and closer, becoming larger and larger. Soon the star will almost be upon you. Now in your own imagination you can visualize that star; it is almost upon you. And now, it is going farther and farther away. It is retracing its path, going farther and farther away into the vast universe. Soon, you will barely be able to see it at all. When you can no longer see that star, you will be in a deep, sound sleep; you are falling deeper and deeper into sleep now. The star is moving farther and farther away. Now you can hardly see it; now you cannot see the star at all. It has disappeared completely, no longer in sight at all. It has disappeared completely, no longer in sight at all. Breathe very deeply . . . very deeply . . . so relaxed and peaceful . . . with each breath you take you will go deeper and deeper asleep . . . so relaxed . . . very good . . . "

THE EYE OPEN-AND-CLOSURE METHOD (FLOWERS' METHOD)

The Flowers' Method of induction was developed by Sidney Flowers, and it is one of the most effective inductions you can use, especially on refractory (resistant) subjects. It employs the use of so much ocular muscular action with its constant opening and closing of the eyes, that sheer muscle fatigue will cause the eyes to remain closed after a short time. As the subject fixes his gaze at a single spot or object, speak to him as follows:

"I want you to look at that spot on the wall. Keep your eyes fixed on that spot. I am going to begin counting. I want you to open and close your eyes with each count. Each time you open your eyes, keep them fixed closely on that spot. I will count from 1 to 20. You will find that each time you close your eyes, they will want to remain closed. Each time you open them, it will be more difficult to do so, more difficult than the last time, much more difficult. By the time I reach 20, or before, your eyes will be so heavy that they will stay closed and you will go deeply asleep. Counting now . . . One, your eyes are open, now closed . . . Two, open . . . and closed . . . Three, open and closed . . . your eyes are becoming very tired now, heavier with each closing . . . Four, open . . . and closed . . . so heavy . . . Five, open . . . and closed . . . so hard to open your eyes, Six . . . so drowsy and sleepy that your eyes just don't want to open, Seven, open . . . and closed . . . Just don't try to open them any more as you take a deep breath and go deeply asleep . . . "

NOTE: You can observe when to tell the subject "not to try any more". It is unusual for the count to go any higher than ten, but in some highly resistant subjects, it can happen. It is up to you to watch the subject and speak to his individual reactions to your words.

USING SOUND

Music. There are literally thousands of recordings which you can use as background music or sound effects to enhance the induction process. These recordings are available as audiocassettes in almost any record or book store. Some of these are classified as "new age" music and provide a background of beautiful, soothing instrumental sounds. Others are classified as "environmental" sounds, and they provide the background sounds that are naturally found in the environment such as a thunderstorm, the sounds of ocean waves or the sounds of a forest. I find that limited use of such recordings is a very effective way to block outside distracting noises and to add a quiet ambience to the general atmosphere. In using them during the induction, you may or may not wish to refer to the sounds. If you do, say something similar to the following:

"As you listen to the sounds of the ocean waves rolling in, rolling out, you just go deeper and deeper relaxed, rolling in . . . rolling out . . . deeper and deeper . . ."

Metronomes. A metronome with a slow beat can be an excellent aid to the induction process. You may produce hypnosis in your subject by saying:

"As you listen to my voice, you begin to relax completely. Listen carefully and you will hear a gentle, regular sound, the ticking of the metronome, the sound will take you deeper . . . deeper and deeper . . . the beat of the metronome is relaxing you completely . . . every beat seems to say deeper . . . deeper . . . deeper. Each and every beat is taking you deeper and deeper to sleep . . . calm, peaceful, relaxed . . . "

Fans or air conditioners. The regular sound of the fans of building heat or air conditioning can provide you with an excellent means to induce hypnosis. Simply ask your subject to relax as you say:

"Close your eyes now and listen to my voice. I want you to concentrate completely on the gentle whirring sound of the air conditioner. Notice how regular, how soft and peaceful that sound is and how sleepy it is beginning to make you as it takes you deeper . . . deeper . . . and even deeper . . . The monotonous drone of the fan just makes you relaxed and peaceful, calming your entire body and mind as you go deeper and deeper still . . ."

THE ARM-LEVITATION INDUCTION

"Put your right hand on the table. I want you to concentrate all your attention on that hand. You can look at it, and I want you to be aware of all of the sensations and feelings in that hand. For example, you are aware that it is sitting on the table. There is weight there. You are aware of the texture of the table; you can sense the position of every finger in relationship with every other finger. You're thinking about the temperature of that hand, as you look at that hand with deep concentration, you are going to notice that one of the fingers in that hand will feel different from the others. It might be the thumb or the little finger, or perhaps the index finger or the big finger, or the ring finger, but one of them will feel distinctly different from the others. And that feeling may be that it's a little warmer, or a little colder, or perhaps it stings a little, or maybe it feels numb, or heavier, or even lighter. As you pay close attention, that particular finger will tend to lift itself up from the table just slightly. Can you show me which finger it is now? Thank you. Very good. Now I want you to concentrate and you will find that the finger is becoming kind of numb, it's sticking straight out, almost as if it were made out of wood. That wooden feeling will start spreading to the other fingers close to it and they, too, will begin to lift themselves and straighten. And you will find that next you will experience a light feeling in the fingers,

and they want to rise as if they were cork floating in water. Imagine now that there is a balloon attached to the wrist of that hand, raising that hand upward in the direction of your face, and it gets higher and higher, higher and higher. And you feel a drowsy sensation as it comes closer and closer to your face, and the higher your hand comes up, the drowsier you feel, and you begin to think that when your hand touches your face, you will go into a deep and profound relaxed state. Now, it is coming closer, and closer, almost touching, almost touching, very good, touching now, as you just feel a sense of peaceful relaxation. And as your hand goes down, you go down, too, into a deep, deep relaxed state, and you feel yourself go down now to a deep, comfortable place of complete relaxation."

DAVE ELMAN'S TECHNIQUE OF INDUCTION

"For the moment, rest your arms limply on your thighs, just like this. Now, I want you to look out here at my hand up in front of your eyes like this. When I do, I'll pass my hand down in front of your eyes. Keep your eyes fixed on my little finger. As I pass my hand down, that will cause your eyelids to close down.

All right, now fix your eyes on my little finger. Now, I'm passing my hand down in front of your eyes, and as I do, let your eyelids close down.

Now your eyelids are closed down. I want you to relax every tiny muscle and nerve in and around your eyelids. I want you to relax them so much that they wouldn't work even if you wanted them to.

Now, when you know that you've relaxed them that much, they wouldn't work if you wanted them to. Test them; you'll see you've been completely successful. Relax them that much that they wouldn't work if you wanted them to. Now, test them; you'll see you've been completely successful. (Pause

3 seconds).

All right, that's fine. Now, stop trying, and just relax and go deeper now. Now, I'm going to raise your hand. I will do it by grasping your right thumb in my fingers like this. As I lift your hand, just let it hang, kind of limp in my hand. Then, when I drop it, let it drop like a wet limp dish rag. When your hand touches your body, as it drops, I want you to send a wave of relaxation from the top of your head down to the tip of your toes. That's fine!

Now we'll do that again with the left hand. I'm going to pick up your left hand, and as I take your thumb, let it hang limply in my hand. That's good; now you're getting the idea. When I drop it, let it drop like a wet dish rag. When it touches your body, send another wave of relaxation from the top of your head to the tip of your toes, and double the present level of relaxation. That's fine!

Now, your body is relaxed and I'm going to show you how to relax your mind. Listen very carefully. The next time I touch your forehead, I want you to begin counting from one hundred backward in this way: One hundred, deeper asleep. Ninety-nine, deeper asleep. Ninety-eight, deeper asleep, and so on. After counting just a few numbers, by the time you reach ninety-seven, or ninety-six, or maybe at the most, ninety-five, you will find these numbers disappearing. You will find your mind has become so relaxed that you'll just relax them out of your mind.

All right, get ready now, three, two, one (TAP) **begin counting. One hundred, deep asleep. Good, slow them down now. Ninety-nine, deeper asleep. Good. Ninety-eight. Fine. Ninety-seven, start relaxing them out of your mind, deeper asleep. Ninety-six, let them start disappearing and fading away, deeper asleep. Ninety-five, deeper asleep. Let them relax out of your mind. Ninety-four, deep asleep. Now let them fade away completely.**

That's fine. You've relaxed your mind; you've gone into

a much deeper state of hypnosis."

COLOR CONTRAST METHOD OF INDUCTION

A piece of plain gray cardboard 5 1/2″ x 9″ is used and on it two strips of paper 3″ x 1 1/4″ are pasted parallel to each other with a space of 2″ between them. One strip, pasted on the right, should be light blue, the one on the left, light yellow. Both should have a dull finish. The subject, lying on a couch, is given the cardboard to hold at arm's length (provided that he has normal eyesight) . . . The subject is asked to look at the slit between the two strips without interruption. While he is doing this, the hypnotist says:

"What do you see exactly on that cardboard?" The subject will naturally reply: "A piece of gray cardboard on which a yellow strip is pasted on the left, and a blue one on the right of it, with a gray slit between." The subject is told, **"As you continue to watch the picture, especially the slit, you will soon observe some additional colors appearing."** (These chromatic phenomena, as a general rule, will be observed by any normal person, including the so-called "red-green dichromatics, and by all anomalors trichromatics"; they consist in appearance of the respective complementary colors along thc outside edges of the yellow and blue strips). The hypnotist should say:

"When you see colors appear it is a sign that the hypnotic state is setting in. The appearance of the colors is proof of the hypnotic influence; it is a kind of fatigue phenomenon of the eyes. In the same way that you see these color phenomena, you will observe some other signs of the approaching hypnotic state.

Keep looking at the slit and you will soon see that the inner edge of the blue strip, that is to say, the edge bordering on the slit, becomes more intensely blue, while the rest of the blue strip will be a much duller shade. In precisely the

same manner you will notice that the part of the yellow immediately bordering on the gray slit, becomes more intensely yellow, while the rest of the yellow strip becomes more faintly yellow. Just keep looking closely . . . keep looking fixedly at the slit . . . look very closely; you will see something else happen as well. You will also see colors appear in the slit; you will see a yellow border appear along the edge of the blue strip, and a blue border along the edge of the yellow strip. These two newly made colors will touch at about the center of the slit; now and then they will overlap; they may even disappear for a moment or two; your consciousness is now beginning to waver, owing to the hypnotic condition.

You remember that I told you just now that, as you observed the color phenomena, you will find that your eyelids are getting heavier and heavier . . . still heavier all the time . . . You will feel that you are getting more and more tired . . . tired and weary . . . and you will soon get so tired that you would just love to shut your eyes. When you feel like that, don't resist . . . You may close your eyes."

DEEPENING PROCEDURES

Once the subject is clearly relaxed and cooperating, there are a number of techniques for deepening his hypnotic state. In general, the procedure for deepening is first to suggest that the relaxation is progressively becoming deeper and deeper, and to allow short periods of silence in order to allow it to happen.

ELEVATOR METHOD

"Visualize yourself in an elevator at the top of a 20-story building. See yourself pushing the button for the first floor, and now the elevator begins to descend. Imagine that you

are watching the numbers over the elevator door, and with each number, you go deeper, deeper, and even deeper. When you reach the ground floor, floor number one, you will be in a very deep, relaxed state, ready to listen and follow the positive suggestions to improve your life. Ready . . . starting down now . . . Twenty, nineteen . . . deeper and deeper . . . eighteen, so relaxed, going down. Seventeen, so calm and peaceful as you go deeper and deeper . . . Sixteen, way down now . . . Fifteen, nothing to distract you as you go further and further down . . . Fourteen . . . Thirteen . . . Twelve . . . so relaxed now . . . Eleven, Ten . . . going even further down, calm and peaceful . . . Nine, down . . . down . . . down . . . Eight, Seven, Six . . . so relaxed . . . Five, nothing to disturb you . . . Four, so deeply asleep, enjoying it so much . . . Three . . . very good . . . Two, deeper and even deeper . . . and One . . . deep asleep now, deep asleep."

REVOLVING HANDS TECHNIQUE

Take the subject's hands and start them in motion, revolving them around and around each other. When the motion is well established, say:

"Now your hands are revolving around and around, faster and faster . . . they keep revolving . . . making circles as they go around and around . . . around and around, it is impossible for you to stop them, and each time you make a circle with your hands, you will go deeper and deeper relaxed . . . around and around, turning and turning, deeper and deeper . . . Try, but you cannot stop . . . Your hands keep going around and around . . . Now they change directions . . . They are making circles the other way now as you go deeper and deeper . . . around and around, around and around . . . They are turning automatically, and you cannot stop them . . . Stop trying now, and as you relax more and more, your hands drop into your lap. When they reach your lap you go one

hundred times deeper, so calm, peaceful and comfortable . . . Very good."

VOGT'S FRACTIONATION TECHNIQUE

The fractionation method developed by Vogt is a very effective method for deepening hypnosis. It, like the Flowers Technique above, is very useful with the refractory subject. It requires hypnotization, de-hypnotization and immediate re-hypnotization. Using the images from the subject's own experience of the first hypnosis, the therapist is able to produce a most satisfactory hypnotic state. With each re-hypnotization the subject is told that he will "go deeper than ever before", resulting in a compounded effort that he will find hard to resist. After hypnotizing the subject, awaken him, and ask him what he experienced at his most relaxed point in the immediately preceding session. If, for instance, he says, "I was walking in a beautiful green meadow," you will incorporate that information in the next induction as you immediately say:

"**. . . And now as you drift back into relaxation, imagine yourself back in that beautiful green meadow . . . and as soon as you see yourself in that meadow, you will go even deeper and deeper relaxed, a hundred times deeper than ever before . . . so calm and peaceful . . .** "

NOTE: This procedure can be repeated again and again until a satisfactory level of hypnosis has been achieved. Vogt's method is effective because it precludes the possibility of the therapist's inadvertent use of objectionable imagery since it uses the subject's own words. It also provides information that can be used for suggestions in subsequent sessions with that subject.

OTHER DEEPENING SUGGESTIONS

". . . And now I want you to imagine that you are taking a stroll. You are strolling through the most beautiful park you have ever seen. It is a lovely day . . . the sky is clear and blue . . . just a few soft, puffy white clouds that seem to move with the light breeze. The sun is shining, warm and pleasant. As you walk, you see two large, beautiful trees, and a hammock is swinging between them. See yourself as you go to the hammock, and as you let your body sink down into the hammock, it begins to swing back and forth . . . back and forth . . . Each swing takes you deeper and deeper . . . back and forth . . . deeper and deeper, so relaxed and calm . . . so comfortable . . . deeper, deeper and deeper . . . back and forth, back and forth . . . "

or:

". . . And now I want you to visualize yourself in front of a blackboard. Imagine that you take a piece of chalk and draw a large square on the blackboard. Now trace it around clockwise three times, around and around, and this takes you deeper and deeper, around and around . . . deeper and deeper. And now, you start tracing in the opposite direction, around and around, deeper and even deeper . . . so relaxed and peaceful, deeper and deeper asleep . . . "

or another "blackboard" sequence you may use:

". . . And now just visualize a large blackboard in front of you. You have a piece of chalk in your hand, and you begin to write the alphabet, one letter at a time, beginning with a large letter A. When you've written your A, you erase it, and you write a large letter B. See yourself as you erase the B, and you proceed to write the next letter C. . . erase it and write the letter D...keep on writing and erasing, writing and erasing, each time you erase, going deeper and deeper relaxed . . . That's right, keep on writing and erasing . . . If you lose your place, just pick up wherever you think you

left off. It really doesn't matter. Keep on writing and erasing . . . deeper and deeper with each letter . . . writing and erasing . . . "

CONFUSION TECHNIQUES

The confusion technique for hypnosis deepening was developed by Milton Erickson, and it is based on giving contradictory instructions and suggestions to the subject. It works well because the conscious mind becomes exhausted at trying to figure out what is being said, and it gives up to the subconscious mind where change work can occur. The statements made must be meaningful, although contradictory, and delivered in such a way that the subject feels that he just simply does not have enough time to make sense out of what he is hearing. A hypnotic lethargy ensues, and hypnosis is then easily established.

For instance, the subject is told that his right hand is rising and his left hand is immobile. Immediately then he is told that his left hand is rising, and his right hand is immobile. The next immediate suggestion is that his right hand is warm, and his left hand is cold, then vice versa. After that, the original suggestions of rising and immobility are given again. These suggestions must be given with confidence in a rapid, insistent manner.

Another way to use the confusion technique is by counting:

"I am going to begin to count now in a different way. As I count backwards from 10 to 0, you will go deeper and deeper, and as I count upwards from any of those numbers . . . you will awaken just a little with each number. Go deeper now as I count 10, deeper . . . deeper . . . 9, deeper and deeper . . . 8, deep asleep, 7, deeper, 8, awakening just a little, 7, deeper now, 6, even deeper still, 5, deeper . . . now 6, waking up just a bit, 7, up a little more, 6, go deeply asleep now, deeper and deeper, so calm and relaxed, 5, feeling

calm and peaceful as you go deeper, 4, deeper, 3, deeper and deeper, 4, waking up so slightly, 3, down now, deeper and deeper, etc . . . "

NOTE: You may make this routine as lengthy as you wish. Because you reverse the signals, the subject finds himself concentrating very hard on what you are saying, and he becomes confused and mentally tired, giving in to the relaxation.

Counting techniques can be varied in many ways to produce confusion. Ask the subject to count to himself by 3's or 7's to 100, then backwards. Or ask him to count ten breaths, and go deeper with each breath, then count three breaths to awaken slightly, then five more to maximum relaxation.

PROGRESSIVE WARM, HEAVY FEELING PROCEDURE

". . . And now you notice that there is a warm, numb feeling beginning to form in your forehead, just above your eyes. It starts to spread over the top of your head and into your face, and around to the back of your head, and you feel a pleasant sensation of heaviness and relaxation. Now it moves downward through your neck, and your neck becomes heavy, heavy, heavy, and this warm, heavy feeling now goes through your shoulders and down into both of your arms and hands. They feel so heavy, just like they might be limbs on the trunk of a tree. And now this warm, heavy feeling moves into the trunk of your body, down through your chest and your abdomen, and drifts down now into both of your legs, your thighs, your calves, and your ankles begin to feel this warm, numb, heavy feeling, and it moves on down to each of your toes as you go deeper and deeper relaxed . . . "

AWAKENING

Awakening the subject is the easiest part of the session. Hypnotized subjects can always be awakened. In my twenty years of experience, I have neither had nor heard of anyone not being able to come out of hypnosis.

The awakening can be performed by simply suggesting to the subject that he is to open his eyes and be wide awake. You may also tell the subject that on a given signal, such as the clap of your hands or the snap of your fingers, he will awaken.

Some subjects will awaken the moment the therapist ceases to speak. Conversely, there are subjects who go very deep (somnambulists) who prefer to take a short nap before they wake up naturally.

Generally, though, I prefer to use a "counting-up" awakening, interspersed with positive post-hypnotic suggestions. This method is effective with 99% of hypnotic subjects.

Let the pitch and tempo of your voice gradually rise as you awaken your subject. Sound sincere and enthusiastic as you say:

"When you hear the number 5, you will wake up feeling better than you have ever felt before . . . One. Getting ready to wake up now, feeling fine, Two. Your mind is clear, and your body is refreshed, Three. Looking forward to each and every day, Four. Ready to follow through on all of your positive suggestions, feeling positively wonderful, Five. Wide awake now! Feeling great!

CHAPTER ELEVEN

THE PHENOMENA OF HYPNOSIS

The mastery of simple induction procedures and the formulations of effective suggestion should be the emphasis of practice for the beginning hypnotherapist. There are, however, innumerable phenomena that occur in hypnosis that can be used to facilitate therapy. Once you have established a solid foundation in the basic procedures, you may wish to expand your therapeutic abilities, in which case you will need a working knowledge of some of these phenomena. The discussions here are by no means all inclusive, but I have chosen specific phenomena of hypnosis that I consider important for any hypnotherapist to know about.

IDEOMOTOR RESPONSES

Ideomotor responses are fundamental in hypnosis, although we all experience ideomotor responses many times each day without any formal induction. Ideomotor activity refers to the *involuntary capacity of muscles to respond immediately to thoughts, feelings and ideas.* Have you ever watched a mother as she spoon-feeds her baby? As she moves the spoon toward the baby's mouth, her own mouth will pucker and open. Or have you ever been a passenger in a car that had to make a quick stop to avert an accident, and notice your own foot pressing on an imaginary brake pedal?

The pendulum experiment you performed in Chapter 4 is technically called "Chevreul's Pendulum Test", and it depends completely upon the involuntary or ideomotor muscular responses of the individual performing it. You may recall how you directed your thoughts in a definite direction. Those thoughts were generated by your conscious mind. However, those conscious thoughts produced a series of events within your body that were controlled by your subconscious mind. Those events in turn caused minute contractions in the tiny muscles of your fingertips which resulted in the pendulum's moving in one direction or another. Because the pendulum movement is in direct response to impulses that are generated in your own mind, it is not, as some would have you believe, a fortune-telling device or technique. Whoever is swinging the pendulum is influencing the answer from the truth as he knows it, even though that knowledge may be on a subconscious level. In my classes, I demonstrate this by asking one of the students to inquire of the pendulum whether or not my daughter's birthday will come on a Monday this year. When the student responds to me with their answer, either "Yes," or "No," I only then tell him that I do not have a daughter. However, since the student had no way of knowing that, he was only giving me a truthful answer as he knew it.

In hypnosis, it is possible to "build in" such reflex responses to generate accurate information from the subconscious mind of the subject. The most common use of this phenomena is the establishment of "finger responses" to answer questions by the therapist. An answer elicited in hypnosis by a finger response is almost always a direct answer from the subject's subconscious mind.

This is useful to the therapist in many ways, not the least of which is to determine the subject's motivation. For instance, you may have a client who says he wants to stop smoking. However, when he is questioned under hypnosis, his finger signals indicated that he subconsciously does not want to quit. If that is the case, then no amount of hypnotherapy will cause him to quit, because subconsciously, he does not want to.

ESTABLISHING IDEOMOTOR RESPONSE FINGER SIGNALS

After the subject has achieved a state of relaxation, ask the subject for permission to speak directly to his subconscious mind. When he has given you that permission, have him determine the fingers to be used for responses from his subconscious. The subject will decide which fingers will signal which responses. Four responses will be necessary: "yes," "no," "I don't know," and "I don't want to answer that now." Say to the subject:

"Now you are completely relaxed. I want you to focus your complete attention on your fingers. Think of the word yes . . . yes . . . yes . . . over and over again until you notice which finger is your 'yes' finger. As you keep thinking of the word yes, you will soon notice a slight pull or tug sensation in one of your ten fingers—let it raise up slightly, and we will know that is your 'yes' finger."

As soon as you observe the finger move, encourage the subject by saying, **"Very good. We know now that your right index finger is your 'yes' finger."** Then say: **"Now repeat the word 'no' over and over, again and again, paying attention to your fingers. When you notice the pull, that twitch in another finger, we will know that one is your 'no' finger."**

When you notice that your subject is moving another finger, again acknowledge his choice by saying, **"I see that your**

left index finger is your 'no' finger. Very, very good." Repeat this procedure, directing the subject to select an "I don't know" finger and an "I don't want to answer" finger.

Once you have established these signals, you are ready to ask the subject whatever you need to know, confident that the answers are coming right from his subconscious mind.

DISSOCIATION

Dissociation refers to the inherent ability of a hypnotized subject to "detach" himself from his environment. This phenomena, like all other hypnotic phenomena, occurs in nonhypnotic levels. We have all had the experience of a reverie state where we were "some other place" than our present environment. This state is similar to dreaming when we "see ourselves" participating in whatever activity is taking place.

Obviously, dissociation has many uses in hypnosis. It is frequently used to produce anesthesia. William Kroger, in his book *CLINICAL AND EXPERIMENTAL HYPNOSIS*, gives us a good example of this use of dissociation. The following remark to a deeply hypnotized patient in a dentist's chair automatically will raise the pain threshold: **"You would not mind going out to the ball park, would you? It is such a nice day for a baseball game, isn't it?"** By causing the patient to mentally transport himself to a pleasant place, his threshold of pain is raised, thereby lowering his anxiety.

TIME DISTORTION

Time distortion refers to the ability of the human mind to estimate time, condense time or expand time. Everyone has an internal "clock" that is capable of making extraordinary judgments regarding time. This, too, is a situation we have all experienced in our everyday waking lives. When we are involved in a tedious situation such as having to endure a long, boring lecture, one hour often seems like three. If, on the other hand, the lecture is stimulating and lively, the hour passes so quickly we can scarcely believe it. A three-hour plane trip often seems to take forever when we are alone, but the time seems to fly by if we are engaged in an interesting conversation with a companion. How many times have you awakened an hour earlier than usual in anticipation of a vacation or some other enjoyable experience? Or how many times have you told yourself before going to sleep that you will wake up at a designated hour, only to do exactly that, often within minutes of the appointed time?

In hypnosis, the natural ability to distort time is increased through hypnotic suggestion. Briefly, 1 minute of experiential time can be equated with 10 minutes of clock time, or something similar, for time expansion. For time contraction, 10 minutes of clock time can be condensed to 1 minute of experiential time.

This phenomenon is especially useful for the client who is suffering from pain, when hours may be made to seem like minutes. Obviously, there are many additional therapeutic applications possibilities for time distortion whenever time contraction or expansion is thought to be beneficial to the client.

Hypnotic suggestions to induce time distortion may be given as follows:

"Every minute of actual time will *seem* like 10 minutes to you. Time will go by very, very slowly, seeming like an eternity. Every 5 minutes that you are in this deep, relaxed and peaceful state *seem* as long as an hour. You will awaken rested and refreshed as if you had a full night's sleep."

AUTOMATIC WRITING

Do you ever doodle or draw on paper while you are listening to a lecture or talking on the telephone? Both occurrences are common, everyday instances of the manifestation of the phenomenon of automatic writing. The written material produced by the hypnotic subject can be very useful to the hypnotherapist, especially when it comes from the client who has trouble expressing himself verbally. Scientific investigation by Wolberg concludes that this is true because graphic activity (writing) is less inhibited by cerebral (conscious) control than even hypnotic verbalization of thoughts and feelings.

In automatic writing, the hypnotized subject may not be aware of what is being written until it is brought to his attention after he has awakened. In fact, while writing, the subject may be conversing intelligently or even reading material on an entirely different subject! This, of course, demonstrates that automatic writing is closely related to, if not in fact the same as, the phenomenon of dissociation.

When using automatic writing in the therapeutic setting, I find it helpful to use a rather large pad of paper and an easy-to-write-with felt-tip pen. Many people write much larger when doing automatic writing than they do in full waking consciousness. This is probably because they often revert to a childish, large scrawl or printed letters.

Explain to your client about what automatic writing is before you induce hypnosis. Tell him what you intend to ask of him, so he will be at ease with the process. Find out whether he is right- or left-handed. After you are satisfied that your subject is sufficiently relaxed, begin by saying:

"As you sit here, you will continue to be relaxed . . . deeply asleep and calm. As I stroke your hand, you will notice that it is becoming numb. You will experience the sensation that this hand is no longer a part of you . . . it is comfortable, and relaxed, but detached from your body . . . It feels as

light as a feather now. I am going to place the pen in your hand now, and as I do, you will find that you begin to write as if your hand were moving along with absolutely no help from you . . . it feels like it is detached completely from your body. Even if the information is painful, it does not bother your hand, because your hand is detached from the rest of you now. It is behaving just like an automatic robot . . . very calm and peaceful and relaxed now, your hand feels like it is being moved by another force . . . Your hand will write only the truth, only the truth. You will not question or even think about what your hand is writing, as you become more and even deeper relaxed."

At this point, you may start asking questions of the subject such as, **"How do you feel?" "Where are you?" "What is happening?"**

Allow sufficient time for him to write his responses, and as he is writing, give him the suggestion, **"After the hypnosis session, you will be able to read and interpret what you have written."** Repeat this suggestion several times, because often the subject will write illegibly or in symbols, and he is the only one who has the information necessary to interpret what he meant when he was writing.

REGRESSION

When age regression is used in hypnosis, it allows the subject to go back in time to review earlier situations or events in his life. Remember that the subconscious mind is a vast computer with memory banks that hold every event, every thought, every emotion and every place that the subject has experienced in his entire lifetime.

While it has been claimed that age regression is possible even to prenatal and neonatal periods, it is not an easy thing to quantify as a standard. My own opinion is that an individual's ability to regress to very early fetal stages varies with the individual. There have been many fascinating studies in regression therapy. Subjects who were given aptitude and intelligence tests at various chronological age levels performed exactly in accordance with the age to which they had been hypnotically regressed. Then, another test was given at the next chronological age level to the same subjects. They performed again at the level to which they had been hypnotically regressed, and they were unable to exceed the level of the regressed age until their ages were hypnotically raised.

Regression is most often used in hypnotherapy to trace a current problem back to its original source. Age regression offers a real opportunity for old behavior patterns to change and for new ways of thinking to be established.

Using this type of therapy sets the stage for strong emotional outbursts as the subject remembers painful events. *For this reason, I feel that regression inductions are best left to hypnotherapists who are experienced and skilled enough to deal with traumatic material as it occurs.*

Properly handled, age regression can uncover memories from another time without the disturbance associated with the original event. With the imagination powers acutely attuned as they are in hypnosis, the subject can observe old emotional patterns, and understand that those old patterns are not useful any more for his life today. This, of course involves an attitude of detachment, or, again, dissociation.

After you have your subject into a deeply relaxed state with a progressive relaxation induction, ask your subject for permission from his subconscious mind to proceed. You can do this through ideomotor finger signals as described in the procedure above. There are two distinct methods of regression inductions, with almost limitless variations on each of them. The first one takes the subject back in specific chronological increments, such as:

"I want you to go back now, to the time when you were twenty years old, deeper and deeper now as you listen to the sound of my voice, you are watching a movie of yourself when you were twenty years old. In a moment, I'm going to count to three. When I count to three, you can begin to describe the movie to me. You can talk easily, describing to me exactly what you see and hear as you watch and listen to yourself at twenty years old. One, two, three, watching the movie now, can you tell me what you see?"

After the subject has answered questions about that particular period of his life, take him back to another specific time, such as when he was fifteen, then ten, etc. This can be quite a tedious, lengthy process.

Many therapists prefer the second, more efficient process, called non-directive hypnotherapy. The highly respected medical hypnotherapist Dr. Irene Hickman, is a pioneer in this type of therapy. In the non-directive approach you, the therapist, ask the subject to rely on his own subconscious mind to find the source of the problem. To accomplish this, you say:

"I want you to go back in time now, back to the time when your problem first appeared. As you do this, your subconscious will begin to do all of the work for you. You don't have to try to remember a thing, because your subconscious keeps perfect records, and it will go back through all of your memories for you, just like it was going through a box of files. If you see something from your past that troubles you, do not try to relive it. Instead, just look at it from the chair you're in right now, as if you were watching a movie. That's right. Just keep going back now, back, back, until you find the time when your problem began. When you find the time, let your 'yes' finger rise just a little to tell me you've found it."

When he signals that he has found the time, you give him the following suggestion:

"Now, in just a moment, I am going to ask you to go through the scene where your problem began. You will watch the scene as if it were a movie, from start to finish. You will see what is happening, you will hear what is happening, just like you would in the movies. When you start to watch the movie, lift your 'yes' finger again, and when the movie is complete, when you have watched it through, lift the finger once more. You can signal now when you are ready to begin."

This method of using dissociated images is also referred to as a "pseudo-regression." You are actually guiding the subject as he views past events in the framework of the present. After the subject has mentally reviewed the scene, ask him if it is all right to share with you what he has just seen and heard. Ask him to use his finger signals to answer you. When there is a "yes" signal, say:

"In a moment, I'm going to count to three, and when I get to three, you can begin to tell me what you saw and heard in your movie. One, two, three . . . "

He will describe what he saw in a thick, heavy voice, speaking as if it were a difficult task. You can ask simple, direct questions, and in most cases, he will answer them. If he relays disturbing information to you, continue to assure him that all of that is in the past now, and that he did the best he could at that time with the resources he had, that he is stronger and wiser now, accepting that the past is gone, never to upset him again. These suggestions should be repeated many times.

The process of regression must be unhurried. If the subject appears emotionally upset as he recalls disturbing memories, the therapist should not bring him immediately out of hypnosis. Instead, use the hypnotic state to pacify and relax him. Give him assuring, calming suggestions, and tell him he is in a safe place, protected from any harm, emotional or physical. His distress will pass quickly with your calming words that the past presents no further problems because it is finished, and only the present and future matter to him now.

ANALGESIA/ANESTHESIA

Hypnosis has become an invaluable medical adjunct as an analgesic and anesthetic. It allows mothers to have painless childbirth experiences. It allows physicians to administer a fraction of the usual chemical anesthetics used in surgical procedures. It allows any individual the opportunity to manage the stressful pain of chronic or debilitating illnesses. It also allows us to control everyday, localized pain.

Hypnotic suggestion actually alters the way that the brain interprets messages of pain. We know that the brain manufactures morphine-like chemicals called endorphins. These chemicals are a major part of the body's natural defense system, and evidence suggests that hypnosis actually allows endorphins to be released, producing a "natural narcotic." We also know that since in hypnosis we develop a direct communication with the subconscious mind, we can assist the subject in enhancing his own healing processes.

Producing hypnotic anesthesia is a relatively simple process, and the phenomena is most effective. However, do not ever treat a client or any other subject for pain control unless that person has had a professional medical release or referral. *Always take the complaint of pain very seriously.* Pain is a necessary part of the body's warning system, often warning of injury or disease. As a hypnotherapist, you have the ability to help your client become pain-free, but you do not have the ability to relieve medical conditions. For example, if a client comes to you complaining of headaches, you have no way of knowing if the headaches are caused by tension or stress, in which case you could be of great service, or if the pain is coming from an existing brain tumor. You would obviously be doing your client a great disservice to remove his headache! Therefore, it is your ethical responsibility to consult with the medical professional before making the decision to continue.

When you have determined that the problem is not organic, you may proceed with one of the many methods used to produce anesthesia or to alleviate pain.

Glove anesthesia is the most widely used method to induce hypnotic anesthesia. Glove anesthesia is induced by the therapist's gently rubbing the back of the subject's hand and saying:

"In a very few moments you will feel that all sensation has gone from your hand. Imagine that your hand is getting numb and insensitive, as if you had put it into a bucket of ice. As you see this in your imagination, you feel your hand developing a heavy, wooden feeling, numb and leathery-like, the sensation beginning in your palm, spreading throughout your hand. I am going to count to three now, and when I reach the number three, your hand will be completely numb. One, your hand is becoming more and more numb . . . Two, you are losing all feeling, all sensations in your hand . . . Three, your hand has lost all feeling. It is absolutely numb and insensitive."

At this point, you can check for anesthesia by picking the hand up by the skin on the back of the hand, lightly pinching it and asking the subject what he feels. When he says, "Nothing," you may proceed. Once anesthesia is produced in the hand, it can be transferred to any other part of the body to have that part become numb and pain-free. For example, to achieve numbness for a dental procedure, you would continue:

"Very good. Now I want you to place your right hand upon your right cheek. Good. Now let all that numbness drain from your hand into your cheek. Your cheek is becoming numb, leathery, wooden, just as if Novocaine had been injected into it. When all the numbness has drained from your hand

into your cheek, place your hand once again in your lap." At the end of the dental procedure, the imagery would be reversed, and you would tell the subject, **"Any time at all that you wish to achieve this feeling, you can use your imagination to do so. You can achieve numbness in your hand and transfer it to any part of your body you wish."**

To achieve numbness in another part of the body, it is not necessary for the subject to physically touch the body part. There are times when that would be awkward and inappropriate. It is just as effective to tell the subject to imagine touching the area he wishes to numb, transferring the anesthesia that way. The results will be exactly the same.

Pain Control is easily accomplished after you have completely relaxed your subject, by using one of many approaches such as the following:

"Imagine that the nerves that lead into ...... (the painful area) are controlled by switches in your brain. See your hand turn the switch that controls those nerves. It turns the switch to "off". As your hand leaves that switch in the 'off' position, the pain is turned completely off."

Or:

"Visualize the pain as a green mist. Now I want you to visualize an opening in your body, right at the point of the pain, and inhale. Very good. Now, as you exhale, see the green mist leaving your body through the opening at the troubled spot. The mist leaves your body, and the pain is gone. It is completely gone, as you continue to relax deeper and deeper . . ."

Another very good way to relieve pain is to place your own hand directly upon the painful area and say:

"Imagine now that my hand is a large sponge, ready to soak up all of your pain. When you give it to me, I will throw it all away, because you just do not need it any longer. Now I am going to count from one to three, and as I do, you will give me all of your pain, allowing me to soak up

all of your pain with my sponge. One, the pain is beginning to leave you now . . . Two, going, going . . . Three, deep breath, and it's gone."

For the professional hypnotherapist, the areas of pain control and management, hypnotic anesthesia and hypnotic childbirth offer unique opportunities for specialization. If these areas are of special interest to you, I encourage you to read some of the many excellent texts that are written specifically on these topics. One of my personal favorites and a classic in the field is Ernest and Josephine Hilgard's *HYPNOSIS IN THE RELIEF OF PAIN.*

HALLUCINATIONS

It is fascinating to note that normal people may produce hallucinations under the influence of hypnotic suggestion. Hallucinations may be positive, where the subject "sees" something that is not there, or negative, where the subject does not see something that is indeed there.

Since in hypnosis, the senses are acute and more sensitive than they are in the waking state, there is virtually no limit to the kind of hallucinations that may be effectively suggested to the hypnotized subject. For instance, a subject may be told that his nose itches, and he will begin to scratch it (kinesthetic hallucination). He may be told that a puppy has just come into the room, and he will bend to pet the puppy's head when told to do so (visual hallucination). If told that he is listening to his favorite musician perform a beautiful concert, he will exhibit the facial gestures that indicate that he is listening with enjoyment (auditory hallucination).

CHAPTER TWELVE

SELF-HYPNOSIS

Voltaire said, "When I can do what I want to do, there is my liberty for me." There can be no liberty to enjoy your life as long as you feel that you are chained to self-defeating habits and attitudes.

When you are motivated to change, you can do so. This is not difficult if your desire is strong enough. The same force which gave you the habit or attitude in the first place can, through hypnosis, be directed to your benefit. After all, we know that the body is only a robot, controlled by the computer-like brain.

CHANGE BEGINS WITH YOU

Remember my original definition of hypnosis as a process which allows you to experience thoughts and images as real. The end result of this process is your own experience of these thoughts and images. It takes place in YOU. The fact is that there can be no hypnosis unless you hypnotize yourself by participating actively and voluntarily in the process. It is true that all hypnosis is self-hypnosis. The therapist is only a guide, or facilitator in that process.

Emile Coué, to whom I have referred in previous chapters, is the discoverer of autosuggestion, or self-hypnosis. You may remember the earlier discussion of his association with the phrase, *"Every day in every way, I am getting better and better."*

Coué, a pharmacist, first came upon his great discovery during his dealing with a man who visited his pharmacy shop frequently, always complaining about this and that vague disorder. One day the man visited the pharmacy, and asked, "Don't you have any new medicine? It is always the same powders and tonics, and they do me no good whatsoever." He continued a tirade of complaints until Coué did give him some medicine. Although Coué knew that there was nothing new or different about the potion, he told the man that it was a marvelous new wonder drug with great healing properties.

A few days later the man came into the pharmacy again, this time excitedly jumping around, shouting for joy, "I'm cured!"

Coué was astounded. He knew that there was nothing new in the medicine. However, to be certain, he conducted a chemical analysis of the "new" product which only confirmed what he already thought to be true: There was absolutely nothing in it that could have caused the reaction claimed by his customer. Coué had discovered the power of self-suggestion, or autohypnosis, and embarked upon a study that would last the rest of his lifetime. He had discovered that what a man believes to be true, generally becomes true.

CAN I HYPNOTIZE MYSELF?

It is my belief that anyone who is not psychotic, retarded or neurologically impaired can benefit from hypnosis. Unless you have one of these afflictions, you can indeed hypnotize yourself.

If you have "lost" yourself reading a book, listening to music, or watching a movie, you have been hypnotized.

If your mind has ever wandered, and you have forgotten for a moment where you were, or failed to hear someone call your name, you have been hypnotized.

If you have ever been so absorbed in a task that you lose all track of time, you have been hypnotized.

My point is, virtually everyone has been hypnotized, or, more accurately, has hypnotized himself. As I said in earlier chapters, *all* hypnosis, whether accomplished with the aid of a hypnotist or not, is self-hypnosis. Your own experience may have been so spontaneous that you were not even aware it was happening, as in the situations described above.

You can learn to use the same state you were in during such situations to become an intentional, self-started and self-controlled exercise leading to the achievement of a desired goal. Teaching you exactly how to employ self-hypnosis for a specific purpose is the reason for this chapter.

While I do believe that any normal person can learn to use hypnosis, I find that there are two important prerequisites to being successful at self-hypnosis: a sincere desire and an open mind.

An open mind does not preclude a healthy skepticism. I ask only that you keep your mind open to the possibility that you can do this, and that you be willing to learn.

THE "WHY" IS NOT IMPORTANT

In previous chapters, I have attempted to shed light on what hypnosis really is, exploring its history and how it works. If these things are of interest to you, please study those chapters. If you choose to expand your knowledge of hypnosis, so much the better. However, the purpose of this section is to teach you how you can put it to work for yourself.

You do not need to know how hypnosis works in order for it to work. Every day we use electricity. Although none of us knows exactly what electricity is, we all use it for light, heat and motion. Someone once wrote to Thomas Edison and asked, "Sir, just what is electricity?" Mr. Edison replied, "Electricity is. Use it."

Hypnosis and its benefits are there for the taking. Use it.

DOES THIS SOUND FAMILIAR?

Amy rises on Saturday morning, feeling wonderful and full of energy. She has all day today and all day tomorrow to do whatever she wants. Some of that time is scheduled away already with an exercise class and a church meeting, but she knows that she can still get a lot done.

She wants to clean out her closet. She wants to take her car in for servicing. She has a new book that she wants to begin reading, and there's a movie playing in town that she would like to see. It's also a perfect time to start on that badly needed weight-loss diet.

She doesn't know it on arising, of course, but during the course of the weekend, she will get started on her closet and get sidetracked by trying to decide what to keep and what to give away. She will leave it unfinished to go to her exercise class, where she will run into a friend who invites her to lunch afterwards. The diet dilemma raises its ugly head as she must decide whether just one piece of chocolate cake could do that much harm. At the service station, the attendant will tell her that she should buy some new tires, and she won't be able to decide whether to go ahead now, or let it go another month or so. At her church meeting, she will be urged to accept a place on one of the volunteer committees. Additionally, her neighbor will ask her for a ride to town, her mother will invite her to dinner, she will be tempted to buy new clothes, and her boyfriend will suggest going to a party instead of the movie.

Amy's weekend sounds ruined before it even begins, doesn't it? What a tangle of dilemmas and decisions! How will she choose? She will probably spend far too much time pondering all the choices, feeling pulled in multiple directions, and eventually coming to a dead stop, getting nothing accomplished, and feeling confused and irritated.

Typical things that she will be saying to herself on Sunday night include, "I never get anything done. I should have gone ahead and bought those tires. I shouldn't have eaten that cake. I don't know what to do about that committee. What is wrong with me? Maybe if I just had more self-discipline . . . If it weren't for my boyfriend . . . If only mother would not be so overbearing . . . If only my job were not so demanding . . . I really have to manage my money better . . . etc., . . . etc., . . . etc. . . . "

Does this sound familiar? Probably so. Most of us know the difference in what we should do and what we actually do. "I know I should lose weight." "I know I should stop smoking." "I know I should go back to school." "I know I should be more patient."

Unfortunately for us, however, knowing is not doing. We procrastinate. We fail to face up to responsibility. We push unpleasant tasks into the background, waiting for "some other time," or "later," hoping somehow that the problem or the unpleasant task will simply disappear. We fall into saying, "I just never get the breaks. I don't understand why I'm so unlucky." We repeat our behaviors and our self-deprecation so many times that they become deeply ingrained habits, at first much more obvious to others than to ourselves. By the time we are consciously aware of these patterns, we are astonished and often overwhelmed at their stronghold on our lives.

Our mind seems to be powerless to carry out our wishes in the endless array of conflicting demands. What sabotages us?

How can you take control? How can you trap these various parts of your mind to make them work together for you?

LEARN TO ACCEPT RESPONSIBILITY

Your current beliefs and attitudes most likely represent a composite of the beliefs and attitudes reflected by the people and things that have been in positions of influence or authority in your life. The pervasive power of the media has undoubtedly had an impact on the way you view yourself and the world around you. Consequently, you may be guilty of looking, as the song says, "in all the wrong places" for the solutions to your problems and for the attainment of your desires.

How often do you say, "I would be happy if only I had ______ or if only I could ______ ?" How about, "If it weren't for ______, I could have a good life," or "As soon as ______ happens, I can ______,"? By placing the responsibility for your unhappiness or problems "out there" on other people or events, you are refusing to look for answers in the only place they can be found . . . within yourself.

The fact is that your life is the direct result of your previous and present thoughts, desires and emotions. Allow me to repeat: **YOUR LIFE IS THE DIRECT RESULT OF YOUR PREVIOUS AND PRESENT THOUGHTS, DESIRES AND EMOTIONS.** Grasp the importance of that sentence! If you take the trouble to watch your thoughts, literally notice what you are thinking every day, you will find that you automatically and undeliberately do a lot of negative "picturing" in your mind. These mental pictures set in motion the forces to cause these "pictures" to actually develop into reality. The ancient dictum, *picture it and it shall be,* is very true. Regardless of how your attitudes and beliefs have come to be what they are, they are yours now. You may wish to examine them at this time to determine if they are serving you in a helpful way. What a wonderful sense of freedom and anticipation you will feel when you accept the wonderful powers of your mind. These powers are yours to create for yourself whatever is necessary for your happiness and fulfillment.

WHAT YOU THINK ABOUT, YOU BECOME

A great philosopher once said, "The ideas and images in men's minds are the invisible powers that constantly govern them." Of course, this is only another version of the old adage mentioned above. We have all heard this same, simple truth expressed a dozen different ways. In the Old Testament, Job says, "For the thing I feared has come upon me." Our fears, our attitudes and beliefs are all imbedded deep in our subconscious minds, and they tend to become self-fulfilling prophecies.

While it is true that what you fear "will come upon you", it is also true that you can create new and positive attitudes and beliefs, and they, too, "will come upon you." You can deliberately create and develop great positive pictures, and bring those about just as well. The most simple and easy-to-understand way to express and remember this is what I repeat countless times in my classes: The body is only a robot, controlled by the brain/mind. What the mind sees, the body tends to do.

SELF-HYPNOSIS—THE GREATEST TOOL

In my hypnotherapy training classes, the primary objective is to teach my students how to hypnotize others. In the process, however, the students learn how to hypnotize themselves. They enjoy it immensely, but more important, they often come back at a later time to tell me what an enormous personal benefit it has been for them, what a bonus they consider that knowledge to be. I personally think that it is the most valuable thing that they take from the class. Self-hypnosis is a lifetime tool. Once you have learned it, you own the most powerful resource for change, for relaxation, that exists, and once it is yours, no one can ever take it from you.

WHAT WILL HYPNOSIS DO FOR ME?

I find it difficult to be conservative in estimating the benefits of hypnosis. There are others in the field that are equally enthusiastic. The English scientist Haldane wrote:

> Anyone who has seen even a single example of the power of hypnotism and suggestion must realize that the face of the world and the possibilities of existence will be totally altered when we can control their effects and standardize their application, as has been possible, for example, with drugs which were once regarded as equally magical.

I am sure you agree with me that the above is a very strong statement, but it is indicative of the respect that many very knowledgeable men of science have for the potential applications of hypnosis.

What hypnosis can do for you depends largely on what you want it to do. Self-hypnosis is inner-directed. You will be giving commands (suggestions) to a computer (your brain/mind) that your robot (body) will carry out and accomplish. Remember that the subconscious mind is a servo-mechanism, a goal-striving machine. Whatever it believes, your body will do. You will be the programmer, and when you follow the simple exercises and directions I am going to give you, you cannot fail.

You generally practice self-hypnosis not as an end in itself, although it is pleasurable. You practice self-hypnosis as a means of effecting a change in yourself. The change may involve a habit you wish to break, a fear you hope to conquer, a chronic state you desire to overcome, or a pain you wish to diminish. You may long to become more assertive and self-confident to your own abilities. All these and more are possible through self-hypnosis.

Actually, even the person who claims not to have a habit he wants to break, a fear he wants to lose or an attitude he wants to change, can still benefit from practicing hypnosis. Who would not gain from a simple, brief exercise that relieves tension and curbs anxiety?

How do you see yourself? It makes sense that before you can improve your self-image, you need be familiar with the one you have.

You may find that you would like to:

- Gain self-confidence
- Build your self-esteem
- Be comfortable with your feelings
- Increase your energy level
- Lose weight
- Stop smoking

Do you suffer any negative emotional state that you would like to rid yourself of? Some of the things we often suffer are feelings of:

- Worry
- Anxiety
- Jealousy
- Inferiority
- Stage fright
- Depression

JUST WHAT DO YOU WANT TO CHANGE?

What is it in yourself that you would like to change? Most concerns, I find, fall into three general categories: habits, emotions and physical complaints.

Each basic grouping, of course, includes a number of specific difficulties. For instance, habits can include smoking, overeating, procrastination, nail biting and other nervous habits. Emotions can include fears, phobias, sadness, depression, anger, irritability, shyness, nervousness and anxiety. Physical complaints might be pain, allergies, insomnia, itching or fatigue. Hypnosis can be effective with all of these ... and more.

Although we do devote considerable attention in this book to gaining mastery over specific physical and emotional problems, that is, eliminating the negative, it is also important to know that you can work on building up talents and attributes you already possess, or accentuating the positive. Positive feelings and attitudes you can engender through self-hypnosis include: love and warmth, tact, poise, courage, and good humor. You can further develop skills of your mind and body such as athletic, mechanical, mental, and creative talents.

SELF-HYPNOSIS IN EVERYDAY LIFE

You may be the type of person who wishes he could feel a little more at ease with other people. You may want to feel more cheerful as you go through what you may consider the monotonous routine of your daily life. Perhaps you could use a boost in your ambition. Self-hypnosis can help you with all of these things.

In the business world, self-hypnosis can be employed on every rung of the corporate ladder from the secretary to the chairman of the board. For the secretary, it can be helpful as an aid in learning and polishing skills. For the executive, overcoming anxiety and developing a positive attitude may be the need.

It can help you improve your performance in sports by diminishing your tension and lack of confidence, and by helping you learn to focus your concentration, self-hypnosis can assist you in reaching your full potential. Similarly, it can be used in learning to play a musical instrument or improving memory.

Another interesting and useful benefit of self-hypnosis is using the phenomenon of time distortion. For example, while in self-hypnosis, you can instruct your subconscious that a few minutes of practice on a musical instrument will bring the same progress that usually comes after an hour of practicing, or an hour's review of material to be covered in an exam will equal a night of cramming. Time distortion can be used in reverse, as well, when you tell yourself that an hour in a boring lecture will seem like only minutes. We know that the Russians, with their advanced knowledge of mind control techniques, teach their cosmonauts to incorporate time distortion to make the time spent in a space capsule seem shorter.

While it is true that you can look to yourself for answers and corrections in most every area of your life, you should never look to self-hypnosis to cure a serious illness without first consulting a qualified physician. Self-hypnosis is not a substitute for medical expertise. Likewise, serious mental or emotional problems require the assistance of a trained professional. If you are in need of a professional physician or mental health care practitioner, contact your local medical or psychological associations.

FOCUS ON ONE THING AT A TIME

I suggest that you focus on one specific aspect of your life over which you want to gain more mastery. There may be several problem areas you wish to confront, but you should deal with them consecutively, not simultaneously. There are two reasons for this:

1. The subconscious is equipped to handle simple, direct suggestions; complicated, multi-part instructions would not be effective.
2. As you overcome one difficulty, you will probably notice improvements in other areas of your life as other problems seem to just disappear. The feeling of strength that comes from one success will likely "ripple" over into other areas of your life. This "bonus" improvement often happens slightly below the level of consciousness, so you will notice it only after it begins to happen.

THE FOUR ESSENTIALS FOR SELF-HYPNOSIS

There are four essentials to achieving self-hypnosis. They are: *relaxation, participation, concentration and imagination.*

RELAXATION

Learning to completely relax is one of the greatest gifts of self-hypnosis. Maybe you are one of the many people who is so accustomed to tension that it has become a habit. (Remember the Law of Concentrated Attention?) Chronic tension is acquired unconsciously and gradually over a period of time. Often the people who have it don't realize how "uptight" they are all the time! Could this be you? You will learn techniques that will allow you to reach total physical relaxation in only moments.

PARTICIPATION

"Of course I want to lose weight . . . I'm here so you can make me do it." When I was doing private therapy, I heard that same phrase worded a hundred ways. "Make me do it," was the message. It simply does not work that way. This is your body and your mind. Total responsibility is yours . . . Keep a cooperative and participating attitude.

CONCENTRATION

Your conscious mind is erratic, flitting about from one topic to the next. It is busy with thoughts, arousing emotions and generally causing distractions by observing and acting on the issues in your everyday life. Mental relaxation is more subtle than physical relaxation; nevertheless, you will learn to quiet your mind so that you can focus your thoughts.

IMAGINATION

Once you are able to envision your goals, your positive expectation of their accomplishment will become a strong, driving force. The anticipation of success will produce the belief and enthusiasm necessary to achieve it. When you are able to create this vision, hold on to it and tell yourself, "I can, and I will achieve my goals."

DEVELOPING YOUR "VISION"

You will find it interesting to note that when you begin to analyze your feelings, they seem to diminish in severity. When you begin to "own" your feelings, you are in control. You are then limited only by your own reluctance to believe in your own capabilities. Your vision of yourself can make you an achiever, an almost-achiever or a loser.

According to Dr. Lewis R. Wolberg, a noted authority on hypnosis and Professor of Psychiatry at New York University Medical School:

> Individuals who relish sensory experiences, or who are able to project themselves into roles, like actors, show a greater aptitude for hypnosis than others. In Dr. Hilgard's laboratory, individuals who had imaginary companions in childhood, who read a great deal, and who had a capacity for immersing themselves in adventure or nature were most susceptible.

IMAGERY EXERCISES

Since your "seeing" yourself as you want to be is the key to the success of self-hypnosis, you must be able to somehow in your own mind, in your own way, create a mental "picture" of what you want. Once again, I refer you to the robot theory. Your body is only a robot, controlled by your brain/mind. Whatever your mind sees, your body will do.

I have compiled that following imagery exercises that will allow you to consciously direct your imagination and sharpen your imagery skills.

MENTAL IMAGERY FOR YOU TO PRACTICE

Exercise: Imagine the following. Note the clarity with which each appears in your mind.

1. A car
2. The face of a friend
3. An elephant
4. Night lights of a city
5. George Washington

6. A camellia blossom
7. Your kitchen
8. The earth from an airplane

MENTAL IMAGERY MANIPULATION EXERCISE:

Imagine the following:

1. Water running out of a faucet
2. Ocean waves rolling in
3. A car passing through an intersection
4. Your friend walking toward you
5. A puppy drinking from a rain puddle

The above exercises are visually focused. Just as visual imagery corresponds to the sense of sight, other types of sensory imagery also result from their corresponding senses.

The next exercise will demonstrate the difference as you notice your experience.

SENSORY IMAGE EXERCISE:

Imagine the following:

1. The sound of thunder
2. A child giggling
3. The sound of a telephone ringing
4. The feel of bare feet on the beach
5. The feel of a warm shower
6. The feel of holding someone's hand
7. The smell of gasoline
8. The smell of a holiday dinner cooking
9. The smell of fish
10. The taste of an apple
11. The taste of Tabasco sauce
12. The taste of peppermint
13. The muscular sensation of pushing a heavy cart
14. The muscular sensation of a brisk walk

15. The sensation of being too cold
16. The sensation of being "too full"
17. The sensation of being very happy

Now, mentally answer the following questions:

1. What color is your car?
2. Where is reverse in your car's gears?
3. How many doors are there in your house?
4. Which door slams the loudest?
5. What color are your mother's eyes?

Doing exercises as these above are fun, and they force you to stretch your "mental muscles".

KEEP A POSITIVE OUTLOOK

To repeat what I said earlier in this chapter, we do not need to exactly understand the functions of hypnosis in order to benefit from its working. There is simply no escaping the empirical fact that the way we think affects the way we feel and the way we behave. The person with a bright, optimistic and enthusiastic approach to life is one who is likely to enjoy success in life. Conversely, the person who starts the day in the dumps, pessimistic about what he may accomplish and fearful of what may befall him, is likely to have a day just like he expects!

If you truly want to make changes in yourself, you are ready now to learn the simple, step-by-step to hypnosis for relaxation and self-improvement.

PREPARE FOR THE PRACTICE

The first thing you should do in preparation for practicing self-hypnosis is to pinpoint the first goal you wish to achieve. It may be a habit you want to break or some other aspect of your life that you wish to alter. (It may be that simply achieving the relaxed state *is* your goal. If so, fine.) For our purposes here we will assume that you want to employ self-hypnosis to effect a change.

Just as you would learn any new skill or game, you should begin by learning the fundamentals of self-hypnosis thoroughly. As you become comfortable with the technique and more adept at practicing it, you will be able to take shortcuts. Having first mastered the rules, you may then mold the exercise to conform to your own needs and personality.

In time, you should be able to use self-hypnosis nearly anywhere, but to learn it most easily and to help you gain confidence in its use, you should start by finding yourself a relatively quiet and secluded spot for practice. An easy chair, particularly one with a footrest or one that partially reclines, is ideal. Whatever the site and situation, you should be where you can be alone and free from interruption. In the early stages when you are learning the technique, you should allow yourself at least 20 minutes for each session. After a few "learning sessions," each experience should become progressively shorter until you take only a few brief moments to achieve total relaxation.

RELAXATION—IT'S PROBABLY MORE THAN YOU THINK IT IS

Relaxation is important for two reasons. One, as an end in itself, it provides a restorative time for both mind and body. The second reason is that relaxation as employed in hypnosis clears a pathway to the subconscious mind, where suggestions can more readily be accepted and acted upon. In his book, *THE ART OF RELAXATION*, Herman S. Schwartz says, "The best results from constant autosuggestion are obtained while we are in a state of thorough relaxation, when the mental "censor" is off guard. Then our thoughts can find their way without hindrance into the subconscious mind."

You may think you already know how to relax, but unless you are one of a very slim minority, you really don't. You may think you are "relaxing" on the golf course or over a game of bridge or even at a movie. Such pursuits are good and even necessary diversions from the pressures and routines of our often stressful everyday lives. However, this is not relaxation as we mean in hypnosis. As we use relaxation here, "relaxation" means the absence of strain or tension. Complete and total relaxation is a state that is easier to describe than to accomplish unless we learn how. That is why it is so important to commit the extra time to your first few self-hypnosis sessions. As I said before, after you have learned the technique, you will be able to put yourself into the hypnotic state in only seconds. You will agree that it was worth every effort.

THE SELF-HYPNOSIS SESSION

The actual self-hypnosis session consists of relaxation, deepening, giving yourself the therapeutic, post-hypnotic suggestions, and the awakening.

RELAXATION—THE FIRST STEP

Complete mental and physical relaxation is required for self-hypnosis. Promise yourself that you will be consistent and persistent in your practice.

Begin by selecting a place that is private and you will not be disturbed by friends, family members, ringing telephones, slamming doors or outside noises. Make yourself comfortable in a chair, a bed or even the floor, if you prefer. Loosen restrictive clothing, and take off anything that might interfere with your relaxation.

Once you are settled in a comfortable position, just spend a few moments freeing your mind of all thoughts. Take a few deep breaths and relax. Let your mind wander. When a thought does occur, recognize it and let it go. Just enjoy the feeling of doing nothing and relaxing.

DEALING WITH A RESISTANT BODY

If your body is resisting relaxation, the following muscle-tensing technique will help. Tightly contract all the large muscle groups: the thighs, buttocks, stomach and upper arms. Deliberately tighten them even more as you think to yourself, *"Tense, tighter, even tighter!"* Then command your muscles to release themselves as you think, *"Now, let go . . . Completely let go!"* Feel your body go limp and heavy like a loose rag doll. See a rag doll in your mind's eye.

Now focus your eyes somewhere in front of you just above eye level. Feel your eyelids get heavy, but hold off closing them until you count backwards from ten to zero. When you reach zero, allow your resting eyes to send a feeling of restfulness throughout the rest of your body.

FOCUS ON YOUR BREATHING

Now, slowly breathe in to the count of five, then breathe out completely to the count of five. Envision breathing in clean, pure energized air, and breathing out all tensions, worries and negativity. Make a suggestion to your body to *let go completely, starting with the top of the head and going all the way down to the tips of the toes.*

The following relaxation transcript can be recorded on

audiocassette tape and played back until you have it memorized. In fact, I recommend taping the entire session for use at first. As your skill is developed, you will say the words automatically to yourself in only a fraction of the time it takes to play the tape, because repeated playings will have enabled you to memorize it easily.

RELAXATION TRANSCRIPT FOR SELF-HYPNOSIS

"My scalp is loose, limp and relaxed. My forehead is smooth and unwrinkled, just like a baby's. My eyelids are very, very heavy as all the tiny muscles around my eyes relax. My face is soft and smooth, and my jaws relax, parting a little. I feel loose and limp, completely relaxed. My neck feels relaxed and free and my shoulders relax, completely free of tension. My entire torso relaxes now, loose and limp, loose and limp. The relaxation spreads down over my hips and a pleasurable feeling of relaxation flows down into my legs, through my legs and into my toes. I feel fine and totally relaxed, free of all outside cares. Now my entire body feels relaxed, from the inside to the outside. I feel no tension, no worry, only a loose and pleasant sense of well-being."

ENJOY THE RELAXATION

Now, let your mind and body just "give in" to the wonderful restfulness as you just breathe deeply and continue to relax. Within moments you will become aware of a sense of feeling "different." Individual experience will vary at this point. Some people report feeling a sense of "glowing", others say they feel as if they are "floating on a cloud", still others report a definite heightening of sensory awareness. Whatever your own personal experience, you are sure to enjoy the peace of mind that comes with this wonderful, complete relaxation. Just remember that it is your mind that will determine how you respond, and you will be reacting to your own experiences and expectation.

PARTICIPATION AND CONCENTRATION

Your mind must be completely clear of distractions before you can concentrate on goals and self-improvement. Once you are totally relaxed, suspend all of your conscious thoughts. Make no judgments. If an unwanted thought intrudes, just gently push it out, as many times as you need to. Do not allow anything to interrupt this, your special time of tranquility.

SPECIAL SCENES FOR DEEPENING

Think now of a restful scene. It might be a day at the beach, in the country, or some special place known only to you. Perhaps you would like to recall a time when you were free of all cares, away from the worries of your daily life. Whatever scene you choose, remember the following points:

1. If you are using a scene from your past, be sure that there are no negative feelings or memories attached to it.
2. Be inside the scene, *e.g.*, participate, rather than observe.
3. The more intensely you can imagine the scene, the more effectively you will really "be there." I recommend that you envision a movie screen where all of your imagery takes place. That way you can more realistically "see yourself as . . ."

You may want to use your own special scenario at this point, but I am including three different ones here that work well:

COUNTRY LANE AND HAMMOCK SCENE

"I see myself taking a walk down a beautiful country lane. The sky is blue and clear, and there is a pleasant breeze gently blowing through the trees. I hear the sounds of the birds, and I smell the fresh fragrance of the lovely flowers that grow wild at my feet. These sights and sounds and smells take the place of all of my concerns and worries, and I feel so relaxed and wonderful. Now, before me I see two tall, strong trees with a hammock hung between them. I stretch out in the hammock, and I watch a few puffy white clouds as they drift lazily by. I enjoy watching their changing shapes as the hammock swings back and forth, back and forth, relaxing me even deeper."

BEACH AND ROCKING CHAIR SCENE

"I am now at a beautiful spot on the beach, just at the edge of the ocean. I am sitting in a rocking chair, feeling the wet sand on the bottom of my feet. I can feel the sun as it warms my shoulders, and I feel a deep sense of relaxation and peace as I watch the ocean waves rolling in, and rolling out. The waves stop just before they reach my feet, and I can see how the water foams as it changes direction, and moves back out to sea. I begin to rock with the rhythm of the ocean, and each wave takes one of my problems, and washes it away to sea. Back and forth, back and forth, all of my problems just washing out to sea, disappearing in the vast depth of the ocean. My mind is free, and I am completely relaxed."

MOUNTAIN LAKE SCENE

"I am now at a beautiful lake in the mountains. The air is clear and fresh, the sounds of nature are all around me. I am comfortably reclining on a wooden dock, enjoying the sparkling blue lake, smelling the fragrance of the pine trees that loom above, listening to the gentle, relaxing sounds the lake water makes as it slaps against wood. I am very still, and totally enjoying this beautiful peaceful place. I can hear the sounds of my own breath, in and out, in and out. How tranquil I feel. As I close my eyes, I can feel the sun warm my face, and I become even more relaxed."

THE THERAPEUTIC POST-HYPNOTIC SUGGESTIONS

At this point, you will give yourself the suggestions to make the changes that you desire. This is highly individualized, of course.

In conveying suggestions to the subconscious mind, picture images seem to be more effective than words. This is because the subconscious mind understand pictures better than words. You must be able to "see" what it is you want to happen. You become the star in your own "movie." For example, if you want to give yourself a suggestion to overcome stage fright, it is not enough to simply suggest, "I am completely confident when I speak before groups." Rather, the words must be reinforced with mental pictures of yourself as a successful speaker, standing in front of a large audience smiling, self-assured and doing an excellent job. You must "see" yourself as successful, and the words you choose for your suggestions will provide your subconscious with the appropriate data to allow those images to occur.

Follow these rules when formulating your suggestions:

1. Condense, revise and perfect your suggestions on paper, and read them to yourself prior to taping your self-hypnosis session.

2. Make your suggestions direct, permissive and positive. Avoid negative words. For example, if you want to alleviate a simple tension headache, it is better to suggest, **"My head is feeling clearer and better, I am becoming more and more comfortable,"** than to say, "Upon awakening, my headache will be gone." You can see that the mention of "headache" is a negative reinforcement of the condition, and there are no word "pictures" to provide the subconscious with the desired effect.

Another example: Do not say, "I am no longer nervous and tense at work." Say instead, **"I see myself at work, calm and confident, doing my job with complete control, etc."**

Emile Coué said, "When you wish to do something reasonable, or when you have a duty to perform, always think it is easy. Make the words, 'difficult,' and 'I cannot,' disappear from your vocabulary. Tell yourself, 'I can, I will, I must.'"

3. Combine the suggestions with your motive for wanting the change. Remember the robot. Picture what it is you want to happen. **"I see myself in front of the mirror, admiring my slim, trim body. I enjoy the compliments I get on my nice appearance."** Or, **"I see myself after dinner, relaxing with a cup of coffee. I feel proud that I am a non-smoker, enjoying the taste of my food more, feeling so good about myself in every way."**

4. Work on one goal at a time. Give yourself suggestions for only one change you wish to make. Plan to repeat the suggestions in subsequent sessions until you reach your goal. When you have reached your goal, or you

know you are well on your way, proceed to the next one.

THE AWAKENING—HOW TO BRING YOURSELF OUT OF HYPNOSIS

After taking yourself into hypnosis and repeating your therapeutic suggestions several times, you may be ready to return to your normal waking state. Keep in mind that you are never in danger of staying "under." You are always in control and can awaken at will, very much like you have awakened many times from a light nap.

After your self-hypnosis session, you will feel invigorated and refreshed. You will notice how sharp and clear your mind is. You will have no bodily tension, nor will you be bothered by negative emotions. To wake up, simply count from 1 to 5, using a positive reinforcement with each count. **"One . . . getting ready to wake up now, Two . . . my body feels rested and refreshed, Three . . . coming up now, Four . . . eyes open, feeling full of energy, and Five . . . wide awake now, feeling wonderful!"**

PRACTICE MAKES PERFECT

Remember, all skills require time and effort to acquire. I suggest that you set aside a specific time each day to practice your self-hypnosis. Commit to yourself that you will be diligent. Know that it will come easily and naturally after only a few sessions, and the results will amaze and please you.

HOW WILL I KNOW IF I AM HYPNOTIZED?

One of the common misconceptions of hypnosis is the one that equates hypnosis with sleep. A person in a deep hypnotic state does indeed appear to be asleep, but only because his eyes are closed, and he is completely relaxed.

YOU WILL REMAIN AWAKE

While you are in hypnosis, you will be fully aware and remain sufficiently conscious to give yourself suggestions. The fact that you remain aware of yourself and all that goes on around you may lead you to wonder if you really have been hypnotized. Your first attempts at hypnosis should result in your becoming wonderfully relaxed. As you acquire increasing skill, you will notice how inattentive you are to everything except your own process.

Many people are surprised that the hypnotic experience isn't more dramatic than it is. They expect something like thunder and lightning, or a "magic carpet ride" feeling. "I couldn't have been hypnotized. I was aware of everything," is a very common observation. Do not expect fireworks. The sensation of hypnosis is most often characterized by a pleasant feeling of tranquility.

The intensity of the experience can fluctuate widely, not only from person to person, but with you yourself from day to day. It depends on your mental and emotional condition at the time. However, even during the lightest hypnotic state, therapeutic changes can occur. Dr. Lewis R. Wolberg stresses,

> . . . even if one goes no deeper than the lightest states of hypnosis and is merely mildly relaxed, one will still be able to benefit from its therapeutic effects. It is possible with practice to go more deeply into a hypnotic state, but that is really not too important in the great majority of cases.

SELF-CONVINCERS

There are several exercises you can do to prove to yourself that you are indeed in the hypnotic state. I suggest that you attempt them only after a few induction experiences.

THE HAND LEVITATION TEST

After you have hypnotized yourself, and you are in a relaxed state of awareness, begin to concentrate on your right hand and arm, or if you are left-handed, concentrate instead on the left hand and arm.

When you first concentrate on the hand and arm, notice that they feel relaxed and heavy. Suggest to yourself and imagine in a full participating manner that the heaviness is disappearing and that the weight is draining out of your hand and arm.

Think, **"All the weight and heaviness of my hand and arm is draining away, and I can feel that they are getting lighter and lighter. They are becoming lighter and lighter, light as a feather, now, so light that they seem to want to just float upwards. My hand is so light, it feels as though it is floating in the air . . . as light as a fluffy cloud . . . slowly lifting into the air. My arm is now bending as my hand floats up, higher, higher, and even higher . . ."**

Continue these suggestions, *feeling* and *visualizing* your hand and arm being light, floating, lifting. It may take several minutes, but with concentration, suggestion and the use of your imagination to feel and visualize your suggestions, your hand will begin to move upward, and you arm will bend to accommodate this movement. The movement is usually slight at first, and sometimes even jerky and irregular, but as you avoid resisting the movement as you imagine the lifting, your hand will begin to lift.

THE YARDSTICK TEST

Another test that you can use which will not only indicate when you are hypnotized, but also tell you how deeply you are hypnotized, is the following:

After you have completed your induction and achieved the hypnotic state, picture in your mind a scale of some sort that shows calibrations such as a thermometer, a ruler or a yardstick. Picture it as being vertical, with the low numbers at the top. If you use a yardstick, the one-inch mark would be up, and the 36-inch mark would be at the bottom. Tell yourself that the first 12 inches represent the light hypnotic state, and the bottom 12 inches represent a much deeper state. Now, picture an arrow that is floating beside the yardstick, pointing to the numbers. Visualize it being at the top, and watch it as it slides slowly down the yardstick and settles to indicate to you the depth of the hypnotic state you have achieved.

THE EYELIDS TEST

After you are in the hypnotic state, close your eyes tightly and suggest to your subconscious mind that when you count to three, you will be unable to open them. Repeat this suggestion several times, along with the suggestion that, **"the harder I try to open my eyes, the tighter my eyelids will stick together, and when I count to three, I will be unable to open them. One, my eyelids are stuck together. Two, my eyelids are glued tighter and tighter. Three, they are stuck tightly together and fixed, firmly joined together."** Keep repeating the words, **"stuck tightly together,"** as you try to open your eyes. When the test is successful, the lids will remain closed, no matter how hard you try.

In this test, as in the others described, you should give yourself the suggestions slowly, and repeat them over and over, thus allowing time for them to become effective. Patience and acceptance of the reality that any idea in your mind will reflect itself in your behavior, will result in your success. If the concept of your eyes being stuck together is your vivid mental "picture," then your eyelids will reflect this in accordance with the principles discussed throughout this book.

You will, of course, be able to open your eyes as your suggestion fades, or when you give yourself the positive suggestions that your eyelids are now free to function normally.

WHATEVER THE PROBLEM, THE PROCESS IS THE SAME

Whatever goal you wish to attain, the basic self-hypnosis procedure is the same. The only thing that varies is the special therapeutic suggestions that you give yourself. In order to arrive at the wording that fits your situation exactly, ask yourself the questions, *"Why do I want this change? How will my life change once I've achieved my goal?"* The answers to these questions will tell you what you should incorporate into the imagery suggestions you create for yourself. Just remember that you are watching a "movie" in your mind, and *you* are the star!

Since weight loss and smoking are the most common complaints, I will give you several specific suggestions that you may use for those particular problems. I will also include suggestions that apply to several additional areas of concern. Use the suggestions provided here to adapt to your own personal program. I wish you well. I know you will be successful.

WEIGHT LOSS

Ask an overweight person if he has all of the knowledge he needs to lose his excess weight. He will always say yes. People with weight problems are diet experts. Really. They have tried them all. Eat less. Exercise more. Simple, right? No. Not at all.

The reasons we overeat are imbedded in our subconscious minds like bad habits. Only through permanently changing those thought patterns are we ever able to make permanent changes in eating behaviors. Self-hypnosis makes this possible.

Many times we confuse hunger and appetite. Hunger is a real need, but appetite is a *habit.* Compulsive overeaters are in an almost constant conscious struggle with their will power to deny their appetite. As we learned earlier, will power just doesn't work. Hypnosis helps by teaching the subconscious new attitudes about food.

Think about your eating habits. When do you eat? What do you eat? How much do you eat? Where do you eat? *How will your life change when you have lost weight?*

Obesity seems to just sneak up on some of us, and by the time we realize it, overeating or eating the wrong foods has become a painfully hard habit to break. When you take the time to analyze your eating habits, you will recognize patterns that will help you pick the appropriate imagery for your personal program. By using self-hypnosis on a regularly scheduled, repetitive basis, you will be able to lose weight, and maintain your weight at a desirable level.

SAMPLE SUGGESTIONS FOR WEIGHT LOSS WITH SELF-HYPNOSIS

"I eat only at mealtimes. I eat slowly and enjoy my food more and more. I know when my body's nutritional needs

are met, and when I sense this, I feel completely satisfied. I see myself wearing my new, attractive clothes, feeling so proud of my accomplishment."

MORE WEIGHT-LOSS IMAGERY:

"I know that nothing tastes as good as thin feels."

"I am faithful to my weight-loss program, and I repeat my self-hypnosis exercise every single day."

"The suggestions I give myself are an increasingly powerful force in enabling me to lose weight and maintain my desired weight."

"I see myself stepping on the scale each morning, so pleased at the number I see. I know that I am in control of my body and my behavior."

"I enjoy my exercise program. It feels so good to have so much energy to accomplish so much."

"I exercise my body at every opportunity."

"I imagine a table in front of me, and I fill this table with foods that are harmful to me, harmful to my body and my emotions. I see myself pushing these foods away from me, pushing them off the table. And now on that empty table, I place the many foods I enjoy that are good for me. I see myself filling my plate with these good, healthful foods, and I see myself eating my meal slowly, savoring each and every bite."

"I see myself healthy and enthusiastic, so proud of myself for taking control of my life."

"Food is less and less important to me now, and I enjoy eating small portions. I can easily leave portions on my plate because I know that I do not need all that food. I really don't even want it."

"Whenever I think of eating, I automatically think of healthful food."

"I see myself as an attractive person, and my positive

feelings grow stronger every day."

STOP SMOKING WITH SELF-HYPNOSIS

Every smoker knows all of the reasons that smoking is not a desirable thing to do. The United States Health Department has given us statistics galore substantiating that smokers die earlier, are more prone to illness, and pollute the atmosphere of those around them. Add those reasons to the facts that smoking is expensive, smelly, dirty and destructive, and you have no problem placing smoking high on the "habits not to have" list.

Still, tobacco users cling to the habit, self-destructive that it is. One of the most difficult aspects of breaking the smoking habit is its tendency to accompany another activity that is relaxing. For example, during coffee breaks or after dinner, a smoker will often light a cigarette. Another common "trigger" for smokers is anything that they perceive as stressful or anxiety-provoking. The cigarette then becomes a "pacifier," an ostensible stress-reducer, even though we know that the physiological responses to a cigarette are not stress-reducing; rather, they cause circulation impairment and increased heart rate.

If you ask yourself how your life will improve when you stop smoking, the answers come easily: You will breathe easier. Your circulation will improve. You will feel less tired and nervous. Your sense of smell will improve. Your cough will disappear. Your heart and lungs will strengthen. You will no longer carry the odor of cigarettes on your body and clothes. You will no longer be the object of glares from non-smokers that are forced to breathe your exhaled smoke.

Think about your own life, and formulate your own personalized suggestions to use with self-hypnosis. You *can* become a non-smoker.

How much do you smoke? When do you smoke? Where do you smoke? Who else is affected by your smoking? Does tension make you smoke more?

It is absolutely crucial for you to "see" yourself as a non-smoker. A non-smoker is a person who chooses not to smoke. You do not see yourself as an ex-smoker, a person who forced himself not to smoke.

SAMPLE SUGGESTIONS FOR STOPPING SMOKING

"I am a non-smoker."

"Because I am a non-smoker, I can take deep breaths without coughing."

"I enjoy exercising more with sustained endurance because I am a non-smoker."

"I see myself at my coffee break, enjoying a cup of coffee, feeling relaxed and enjoying the company of my friends."

"I see myself at a party where someone comes up to me and offers me a cigarette. I say, 'No, thank you,' because I am a non-smoker."

"I am proud of learning to use the power of my own mind to rid myself of that worthless habit. I respect my body, and I take good care of it."

"When I feel stress, I close my eyes and breathe deeply ten times. I shift my attention to a constructive activity that I enjoy."

"When I am driving, I relax and concentrate on what I am doing, feeling good about being in control."

"I find the taste of food more pleasurable, and I eat good, nutritious food without gaining weight."

"The smell of flowers and perfumes is more distinctive to me now."

"My mouth is clear of smoke, and my breath is fresh. My clothes and hair smell good, now that I am a non-smoker."

ADDITIONAL SELF-HYPNOSIS SUGGESTIONS

The following suggestions are generalized and meant to be a guide for you in formulating your own therapeutic suggestions. It is up to you to provide the personal imagery that only you can. Take the time to select the images that will allow you to become emotionally involved in this "movie" on the screen of your mind.

FOR SELF-CONFIDENCE

"I am becoming more self-assured, more self-confident every day. I am increasingly aware of my abilities and my potential. I see myself as a worthy and capable person. Through my self-hypnosis exercises, I am learning to tap the power of my subconscious. My self-esteem grows every day. I feel the surge of inner power."

FOR SALESMANSHIP

"I make twenty percent more cold calls every day. I have enthusiasm, and I convey this to my customers. I make my presentations interesting and exciting. When a customer rejects my products (or services), **I become stimulated and motivated to go right on to the next prospect. I am becoming more skillful at my profession every day."**

FOR STAGE FRIGHT

"I see myself standing before a large audience, fully prepared and confident. I am in control and master of my situation. I feel fully assured and my mind works clearly

and sharply. My thoughts flow freely, and I am calm and composed. Success in public speaking gives me a feeling of satisfaction and accomplishment."

FOR FATIGUE

"I feel more energy and vitality each and every day. Even at the end of the day, I remain fresh and full of enthusiasm for life. I enjoy exercise and proper diet because I know that my body responds to good care. I produce more work now with less expenditure of energy than ever before. My supply of physical and mental resources is seemingly limitless.

FOR OVERCOMING SHYNESS

"I become more outgoing every day. I am interested in other people and events outside of myself. My attention is focused externally. I derive pleasure and excitement from dealing with others. I tend to forget myself in my interest and concern for others."

INCREASING CREATIVITY

"I am pleased to be tapping the powers of my subconscious and becoming aware of my abilities and talents. I am increasingly able to bring these talents to the surface. I am able to create periods of inspiration at will. My creative forces are at work, and ideas come to me easily and freely. Any dormant abilities that I may have are steadily emerging from my subconscious so that I can use them at will."

FOR IMPROVING MEMORY

"My memory improves steadily every day. My memory for (names, faces, events, etc.) **is steadily improving. The speech that I am about to study will become committed to memory easily, and I can recall it at will. My mind "works clearly and sharply, and I retain everything I learn."**

or

"I see myself opening a book. I enjoy devouring the material in the book. My mind is active as I flip the pages, and all of the facts, figures and details leave the book and file themselves away in the computer of my mind, ready to be called forth whenever I wish. My mind is brimming with information, and I have a tremendous feeling of self-satisfaction. Memory is becoming one of the attributes I pride myself on, and people compliment me on my memory with increasing frequency. I am able to effortlessly recall facts, figures, events, names and faces whether in conversation or in my own reflection."

EFFICIENCY

"I see myself at my desk, disposing of whatever there is in order of importance. If the phone rings, I suggest to the caller that I return the call later, unless it is of greater importance. I stay at my desk until I have completed the tasks I have set for myself."

ANXIETY RELIEF

"This pleasant relaxed experience I am having now will gradually come to be characteristic of me. I see myself going about my daily life with confident composure and a feeling

of inner calm. Whenever something happens that causes me to feel tension, I temporarily stop whatever I am doing, inhale deeply, and then slowly exhale. As I exhale, I will experience an inner calm and feel a sense of confident composure as it flows throughout my body."

FINGERNAIL BITING

"Each time my hands go near my mouth, I have an instant awareness and insight into the automatic habit that is beginning. I see myself stopping that action, and feeling good about my ability to avoid biting my nails. Whenever I feel tension, I just take a deep breath and slowly exhale because I know that this enables me to relax and be free of those anxious feelings. I am pleased with myself for being in control of my life and my actions."

INSOMNIA

"When I slowly count to five, I will drift off into a peaceful night's sleep from which I will awaken relaxed and refreshed in the morning. Counting now, one, drifting, gently deeper and deeper, two, deeper, drowsy now, three, way down now, three, so peacefully sleepy, four, drifting into sleep, five..."

SPORTS IMPROVEMENT

Sample suggestions for golf:

"Each time I take a club from my bag, I feel confident of my choice and confident in my ability to do well. I see myself preparing for each shot with a practice swing, using my imagination to vividly picture myself completing the swing

of the club with superb form, visualizing the ball going exactly where I have determined it will go. And I will recall and experience that wonderful feeling that accompanies my best performance."

IMPROVED SOCIAL SKILLS

"I see myself meeting with other people. I notice that I am more relaxed and friendly, listening to their names, and making it a point to repeat their names several times as I talk with them. When I have opportunities to participate in activities with others, or when I am asked to share responsibility in a group, I accept with pleasure, when time permits, and I participate with enthusiasm. My social confidence grows day by day. I feel more and more comfortable with the opposite sex. In times of stress or conflict, I remain inwardly calm and seek ways to neutralize negative influences so that I will be effective in promoting constructive relationships. I am proud of my ability to relate myself and my ideas to the interests and needs of others."

IMPROVED PERCEPTION

"I am increasingly attentive to what I observe. I see myself at work, paying particular attention to what is happening around me, watching carefully and listening closely. I am increasingly attentive and alert to what is said to me. I am able to think clearly, and when I am confronted with problem situations, I am able to deal with them in a logical manner."

DECISIVENESS

"When I am confronted with choices, I calmly weigh each one and confidently choose the one best for me. I complete the decision-making process by acting upon my choice. After I consider my options, I have the courage of my convictions. I enjoy the sense of freedom and competence that comes from my increased self-confidence."

APPENDIX

THE HYPNOTIC INDUCTION PROFILE (HIP)

The Hypnotic Induction Profile was developed by Herbert Speigel, M.D., and David Spiegel, M.D. Using the HIP involves filling out a profile sheet based on certain indicators. It is described by its authors as "an objectively scorable, interpersonal hypnotic interaction which also serves as an induction technique." For further information on this I refer you to their book, *TRANCE AND TREATMENT: CLINICAL USES OF HYPNOSIS.*

THE HYPNOTIC INDUCTION PROFILE

Four Phases for Measurement of the HIP

The 4 phases	Items that tap the 4 phases	
1. Preinduction—Pretrance or preceremonial; state of customary awareness	Up-Gaze*	(Item A)
2. Induction—Ceremony for entering formal trance with eye closure —Instructions for postceremonial responsivity; exit the formal trance with eye opening	Eye-Roll Sign	(Items B,C, & D)
3. Postinduction—Postceremonial trance with open eyes; postceremonial responsiveness or experience tapped by Items F-J	Tingle* Dissociation Signaled Arm Levitation	(Item F) (Item G) (Item H)

	Control Differential	(Item I)
—Exit total program with examiner's touching of subject's elbow	Cut-off	(Item J)
4. Postinduction—After trance, state of customary awareness; retrospective aspects of the trance experience	Amnesia*	(Item K)
	Float	(Item L)

**Denotes that recording a score for this item is optional*

The Items of the HIP Induction Scale

Dissociation	"Spontaneous," uninstructed. Score positive (1 or 2) if subject reports that the arm used in the preparatory levitation task feel "less a part" of the body than the other arm, or if that hand feels "less connected to the wrist" than the other hand.
Signaled Arm Levitation	Score positive if, on the instructed signal, the arm rises to upright position. Positive scores vary from 1-4, depending on the number of verbal reinforcements necessary.
Control Differential (CD)	"Spontaneous," uninstructed. Score positive (1 or 2) if subject feels less control over the arm used in the Lev item. The examiner's questions do not indicate which arm is expected to be less controllable.
Cut-off	Score positive (1 or 2) if, on instructed signal, subject reports normal sensation and control returning to arm used in Lev item.
Float	Score positive (1 or 2) if subject reports having felt the instructed floating sensation during the administration of the Lev item.

Hypnotic Induction Profile Score Sheet

Name ______________________ Date __________

Sequence ☐ Initial ________ Previous ________ When ________

Position of Subject ☐ Standing ___________ Supine ___________

Chair ___________ Chair-Stool ___________

Item			
A	*Up-Gaze*	*0-1-2-3-4*	
B	Roll:	0-1-2-3-4	
C	Squint:	0-1-2-3-4	
D	Eye-Roll Sign (roll and squint)	0-1-2-3-4	
E	*Arm (R-L) Levitation Instruction*	*0-1-2-3-4*	
F	*Tingle*	*0-*	*-1-2*
G	Dissociation	0-	-1-2
H	Levitation (postinduction) no reinforcement	3-4	
	1st "	2-3	
	2nd "	1-2	*Smile* _____
	3rd "	1-	
	4th "	0-	*Surprise* _____
I ____	Control Differential	0-	-1-2
J ____	Cut-Off	0-	-1-2
K	*Amnesia to Cut-off or No-Test* _______	*0-*	*-1-2*
L	Floating Sensation	0-	-1-2

Summary Scores

______ Induction Score Profile Score 0-1-2-3-4-5

______ Soft ______ Zero ______ Intact

______ Minutes ______ Decrement ______ Special Zero ______ Special Intact

DAVIS AND HUSBAND SUSCEPTIBILITY SCORING SYSTEM

In 1931, L.W. Davis and R.W. Husband worked out a point scoring system which is included here because it is still often referred to in hypnosis literature.

Depth	*Score*	*Objective Symptoms*
Insusceptible	0	
Hypnoidal	2	Relaxation
	3	Fluttering of lids
	4	Closing of eyes
	5	Complete physical relaxation
Light trance	6	Catalepsy of eyes
	7	Limb catalepsies
	10	Rigid catalepsy
	11	Anaesthesia (glove)
Medium trance	13	Partial amnesia
	15	Posthypnotic anaesthesia
	17	Personality changes
	18	Simple posthypnotic suggestions
	20	Kinaesthetic delusions; complete amnesia
Somnambulistic trance	21	Ability to open eyes without affecting trance
	23	Bizarre posthypnotic suggestions
	25	Complete somnambulism
	26	Positive visual hallucinations, post-hypnotic
	27	Positive auditory hallucinations, post-hypnotic
	28	Systematized posthypnotic amnesias
	29	Negative auditory hallucinations
	30	Negative visual hallucinations; hyperaesthesias

LE CRON-BORDEAUX SCORING SYSTEM FOR INDICATING DEPTH OF HYPNOSIS

The Le Cron-Bordeaux scale is similar to the Davis-Husband scale. It is divided into six divisions rather than five. Two points are given for each symptom exhibited and the total score indicates the depth level. From 14 to 36 points indicates a light state of hypnosis; 38 to 54 a medium state; 56 or more a deep, somnambulistic state.

Depth		*Symptoms and Phenomena Exhibited*
Insusceptible	0	Subject fails to react in any way
Hypnoidal	1	Physical relaxation
	2	Drowsiness apparent
	3	Fluttering of eyelids
Depth		*Symptoms and Phenomena Exhibited*
	4	Closing of eyes
	5	Mental relaxation, partial lethargy of mind
	6	Heaviness of limbs
Light trance	7	Catalepsy of eyes
	8	Partial limb catalepsy
	9	Inhibition of small muscle groups
	10	Slower and deeper breathing, slower pulse
	11	Strong lassitude (disinclination to move, speak, think or act)
	12	Twitching of mouth or jaw during induction
	13	Rapport between subject and operator
	14	Simple posthypnotic suggestions heeded
	15	Involuntary start or eye twitch on awakening
	16	Personality changes
	17	Feeling of heaviness throughout entire body
	18	Partial feeling of detachment
Medium trance	19	Recognition of trance (difficult to describe but definitely felt)
	20	Complete muscular inhibitions (kinaesthetic delusions)

Depth		*Symptoms and Phenomena Exhibited*
	21	Partial amnesia
	22	Glove anesthesia
	23	Tactile illusions
	24	Gustatory illusions
	25	Olfactory illusions
	26	Hyperactivity to atmospheric conditions
	27	Complete catalepsy of limbs or body
Deep or somnam- bulistic trance	28	Ability to open eyes without affecting trance
	29	Fixed stare when eyes are open; pupilary dilation
	30	Somnambulism
	31	Complete amnesia
	32	Systematized posthypnotic amnesia
	33	Complete anaesthesia
	34	Posthypnotic anaesthesia
	35	Bizarre posthypnotic suggestions heeded
	36	Uncontrolled movements of eyeballs—eye coordination lost
	37	Sensation of lightness, floating, swinging, of being bloated or swollen, detached feeling
	38	Rigidity and lag in muscular movements and reactions
	39	Fading and increase in cycles of the sound of operator's voice (like radio station fading in and out)
	40	Control of organic body functions (heart beat, blood pressure, digestion, etc.)
	41	Recall of lost memories (hyperamnesia)
	42	Age regression
	43	Positive visual hallucinations; posthypnotic
	44	Negative visual hallucinations; posthypnotic
	45	Post auditory hallucinations; posthypnotic
	46	Negative auditory hallucinations; posthypnotic
	47	Stimulation of dreams (in trance or posthypnotic in natural sleep)
	48	Hyperaesthesias
	49	Color sensations experienced
Plenary trance	50	Stuporous condition in which all spontaneous activity is inhibited. Somnambulism can be developed by suggestion to that effect.

PROGRESSIVE RELAXATION III

"Make yourself comfortable. Let your hands rest easily in your lap or on the arms of the chair. Close your eyes, and think of your whole body growing limp and relaxed."

"Think of the muscles in the scalp and forehead growing very comfortable and relaxed. You will find as you think of these muscles relaxing, they will do so."

"As the muscles of the forehead relax, you may notice a slight increase in tension around the eyebrows. Concentrate on the eyebrows, and all around the eyes, and this tension will fade away. Feel the tiny muscles of the eyelids relax, and let the relaxation move deeply inside the eyes and deep in back of the eyes."

"Let all the facial muscles relax; over the cheekbones and the cheeks; the jaw and the chin; the lips and mouth ... relax. Let the relaxation move deep inside the mouth. As the muscles of the mouth relax, you will find that your mouth automatically becomes not too moist, not too dry, but just moist enough to keep you perfectly comfortable."

"Feel the relaxation spread deep in back of the throat; deep in back of the head and neck; deep into the neck and shoulders."

"Let the arms relax. Relax the upper arm. Concentrate on the forearms and feel them relax. All the muscles between the elbows and the wrist relax. Feel relaxation spreading across the tops of the hands and deep into the hands ... Deep through the hands to the palms. Now the fingers relax ... All the way to the finger tips. As the fingers relax, you may or may not experience a slight tingling in the fingers. If you do, you will find it to be a very pleasing sensation ... A very pleasant tingling in the fingers."

"Bring your attention back again to the relaxed muscles of the neck and shoulders. Let the relaxation flow into the chest and lungs. Your breathing is easy and gentle. You feel yourself relaxing more and more with each gentle and easy breath."

"You relax more and more with each sound of my voice. All outside sounds are unimportant. You will not allow any outside sounds to interfere with your relaxation. Only the sound of my voice is important now."

"Let the relaxation spread into the broad of the back. Feel it move gently down the back to the small of the back. Let all the muscles of the body go to sleep, in a sense, while remaining perfectly conscious, aware, and concentrating. Feel the relaxation spreading around and deep into the sides. Let the muscles of the abdomen relax ... spreading deep into the sides. Let the muscles of the abdomen relax ... deep into the abdomen. All the muscles of the abdomen and hips, relax. Now let the legs relax. Feel the relaxation spreading into the thighs and knees. The calves of the legs relax, all the way to the ankles. Now let the feet relax. The heels of the feet; the undersides of the feet; deep through the feet to the tops, and finally, even the toes relax. It feels so good to relax, and let go of all tension and care."

PROGRESSIVE RELAXATION IV

"Now that you feel safe and comfortable, I'd like you to close your eyes and keep them closed until I tell you to open them. Just let your body relax ... nice and easy ... Now I'd like you to take a real good deep breath and hold it ... Now let it out s-l-o-w-l-y ... Good ... Now I'd like you to take another real deep breath ... fill your lungs up real deeply and let it out s-l-o-w-l-y again ... Now I'd like you to take one more good deep breath, fill your lungs up real deeply now ... and hold it ... now let it out slow, and already you can feel your body starting to relax ... let that warm, wonderful feeling of relaxation flow all the way *down* to your feet ... feel your feet becoming very loose and limp ... let this relaxation flow up into your ankles ... from your ankles up all the large and small muscles of your legs to your knees ... from your knees now into your thighs ... from your thighs into your hips ... from your hips now into your abdomen, and with each breath you exhale just let your body go *deeper* and *deeper* relaxed ... just let it all go, more and more ... let that warm, wonderful feeling of relaxation flow up all the muscles of your back ... let all the muscles of your back go loose and limp, like a rag doll ... let this relaxation flow up into your shoulders ... now over your shoulders and *down* into your chest, all the muscles of your chest relaxed, all the muscles around your chest relaxed ... just let that warm wonderful feeling of relaxation flow down your arms to your elbows, from your elbows to your wrists ... from your wrists into your hands, going out to the ends of your fingertips, guiding you deeper and deeper relaxed, just letting it all go more. Let that warm, wonderful feeling of relaxation flow up all the muscles of the neck ... let all the muscles of your neck go loose and limp ... let this relaxation flow up into your head. Now, over your head and down into your brow . . . all the muscles of your eyes relaxed, all the muscles around your eyes relaxed . . . all the muscles of your cheeks relaxed . . . all the muscles of your chin relaxed . . . now if your teeth are clenched, just unclench them now, and let your jaw sag, just let it all go, more and more . . . deeper and deeper relaxed . . . now I'm going to count from three down to one, on each count just allow yourself, let yourself go deeper and deeper relaxed . . . three, going deeper and deeper . . . two, going deeper and deeper relaxed . . . one, so deep, so comfortable, so relaxed, just letting yourself go, more and more . . . outside noises will not disturb you in any way, in fact any you might hear will help to guide you deeper into relaxation . . . always letting go, more and more, loose and limp . . . Now I'm going to count from five down to one, on each count let the relaxation double through your whole body . . . five, relaxation starting to double . . . four, relaxation doubling more and more . . . three, very comfortable, very relaxed . . . two, relaxation now almost double in your body . . . one, relaxation now has doubled in your body, every nerve, every tissue, every fiber, doubled in its relaxation, more and more, deeper down, letting go, further and further . . . now I'm going to count from five to one again, and on each count you'll triple the relaxation in your body . . . five, relaxation starting to triple . . . four, relaxation becoming deeper and deeper . . . three, very comfortable, very relaxed . . . two, relaxation almost triple in your body . . . one, relaxation now has tripled in your body, every nerve, every tissue, every fiber, so relaxed. You feel yourself just really letting go, unwinding, loosening up, limp, very relaxed . . . all discomforts now completely gone from the body . . . all your organs are functioning perfectly, all your glands are functioning perfectly, just letting yourself go, more and more . . . "

"You find that your legs and your arms are very heavy,

very comfortable, very relaxed. They are so heavy, so comfortable, so relaxed, if I should ask you to lift a leg or an arm, you will find that they are so heavy, so relaxed, that you do not feel like lifting them, you find that they feel so much better just resting right where they are . . . Nevertheless, I would like you to try to try to lift your leg or arm. (*pause* . . .) All right, stop trying and let it relax . . . it feels so much better to let it relax right where it is . . . " "Now I'm going to count from one to five . . . on the count of five you will open your eyes feeling good, wonderful in every way . . . one, coming up now with all good thoughts . . . two, coming up more and more, with happy wonderful, contented, wonderful thoughts . . . three, coming up more and more, feeling so good, so wonderful, your confidence growing, your respect for yourself growing, your love for yourself expanding more and more . . . four, feeling so good, looking forward to each day with renewed enthusiasm, a greater determination, a greater respect for yourself than you've ever had, coming up more and more now . . . five, EYES OPEN, feeling wonderful, terrific, and at peace with yourself in every way. You do feel wonderful, comfortable, and refreshed . . . Wasn't that a wonderful feeling!"

REPETITIVE MOVEMENT INDUCTION

"Place your elbow on the table with your forearm up like this. Now I want you to stare at that hand while I move it up and down. Up—down, up—down, up—down. As you stare at that hand you will notice a tendency for your eyes to become heavier and heavier, as if they might want to close. Keep staring while the hand continues to go up—down, up—down, up—down."

"You will also notice that the movement in this hand is becoming more and more automatic. It is as if the hand itself wants to move up and down without your doing anything about it. Up—down, up—down, up—down. Your eyes are getting so very heavy that they are gradually closing while the hand is moving more and more by itself. Up—down, up—down, up—down. Now the movement of the hand is so automatic that it keeps going up—down, up—down, up—down all by itself and it doesn't need any more help from me to continue its movement. Up—down, up—down, up—down."

"It is now becoming so automatic that it continues to move all by itself without any control by you. Up—down, up—own, up—down. It seems to be almost outside you with a will to move up and down independently of you. It controls its own actions. You do not control them."

"As it goes automatically up and down, it seems to be saying to you "Deep—relax, deep—relax, deep—relax. Up—down, deep-—relax, up—down, deep—relax, up—down, deep—relax." You are going more and more into a deep and profound state of relaxation. Your eyes are closed. Your head is heavy. It is nodding forward, and you are going deeper and deeper and deeper."

"I will take the hand now and stop its movement. As I bring the hand down you will go down with it, deeper and deeper." *(Soften your voice)*

"Deep . . . deep . . . deep . . . deep . . . deep."

HYPNOTHERAPY SCRIPT FOR ASSERTIVENESS

"...And as you go deeper and deeper into relaxation now, I want you to see yourself as a much more assertive person, able to say No when you mean No. Able to stand up for your own rights. Always polite and kind, but able to say No when you mean No. Make your thoughts known so that you can tell people what you're thinking. Letting people know that you have a mind and can speak up for yourself. Changing the things in your life that you want to change, understanding those which you cannot change and knowing the difference. If you want to change something, you are able to tell those around you exactly how you feel about it, always in a kind, polite manner, making your point. See yourself now in a discussion with someone able, to say to that person, 'No, I think you're wrong,' Listening to his point of view, able to change your mind when necessary, but being able to say exactly what's on your mind, whether it's a professional, business, or personal situation. Making yourself known. Letting people know you have a mind. Letting people know that you think, relaxed and calm about it, handling any situation that comes your way with your abilities and intelligence. Seeing yourself as a worthwhile, intelligent person, with much to offer this world. Able to say what's on your mind."

HYPNOTHERAPY SCRIPT FOR GOOD HEALTH

" ... And as you continue to drift on down and deeper to sleep, you are realizing that your thinking has a profound effort upon your health. Your thoughts can and do affect your general well being, so where you previously thought of yourself as unhealthy, you now replace those negative thoughts with positive ones of radiant health, youth, vim, vigor and vitality, immensely enjoying all that life has to offer. Realizing that illness, both real and imagined, can result from life's day to day stresses if they apply to you, and you tackle those areas of your life that could stand some improvement with confidence, vigor and resolve, applying all of those principles of peace and relaxation that you learned on this tape to all of the areas of your life, to help you become a more calm, healthy, and relaxed person. If you have a symptom that is painful, chronic or frightening, you resolve to go to a doctor. If you doubt the doctor's diagnosis, you get a second or even a third medical opinion. And if the doctors can find nothing major wrong but your conviction that you are ill persists, you consider very seriously the possibility that you are mentally exaggerating or imagining the seriousness of your symptoms. If you recognize yourself as being obsessed about a worrisome illness that your doctors cannot diagnose and cannot cure, and if you do not enjoy such stress, you realize that you can do something about it. You are determined now to start building a lifestyle that provides you with nurturing attention, personal achievement, and other satisfactions in your everyday life that will make it unnecessary for you to continue to hide yourself in sickness. Your subconscious mind is now directed to produce whatever chemical is necessary to heal your body. Each and every day, in every conceivable way, you grow more relaxed, feeling younger, having more energy and feeling better than the day before. Your joints are flexible and comfortable. Your immunization system works as it should to keep you free from diseases. Your arteries are soft, normal and pliable as the blood rushes through them carrying the healing and life-giving elements of oxygen. Your blood pressure remains normal and your heart beats strong and rhythmically. You realize now that the Creator has presented you with the world's most wonderful machine, your own body. This miracle machine has its own non-stop motor, the heart; its own fueling system, the digestive tract; its own filtration system, the kidneys; its own thinking system, the brain; its own temperature control, the sweat glands; indeed this most remarkable contrivance even has the power to reproduce itself. And so you take extra special care, you take extra special attention for your body, and your physical, mental and emotional well-being. And because of this you find yourself applying certain habits to your every day life. You're resolved to devote a portion of each day to improving your health; you devote a portion of each day to improve your mind also, and each and every day you find yourself engaging in some form of moderate exercise and enjoying it so very, very much. You are also going to see to it that you go to bed at a regular, reasonable hour so that you get your required rest and sleep. You find yourself eating good, wholesome foods, and you don't overeat and you don't overindulge in foods that you know aren't good for your health. And while you're eating you can imagine and think of the rejuvenating power that the minerals and vitamins in your food will release in your glands and organs. And you can imagine this very power at work on you. And when you breathe, you breathe deeply, feeling the life-giving qualities of the air flooding every cell tissue. You can actually see this life, filling your entire body, knowing that these things are happening each and every moment of each and every day. You also find yourself observing common sense rules about cleanliness, and if you must smoke, you resolve to smoke in moderation. You never allow drinking to become a problem.

You use discretion as to how many drinks you have. And realizing that an ounce of prevention is worth a pound of cure, you resolve to consult your dentist and physician for periodic check-ups. And you're also going to take time each and every day for some form of recreational relaxation, to balance your day with work and play, developing more and more new habits that are conducive to making you think better and feel better, becoming the person you want to be, can be and deserve to be. Each and every day, in every conceivable way, your health gets better and better. You no longer accept negative attitudes that detract from health. You are adaptable and changeable when necessary. You constantly visualize, imagine and conceive of yourself as being in perfect health. Always radiating youth, vigor and vitality."

HYPNOTHERAPY SCRIPT TO CONQUER PROCRASTINATION

"... And as you continue to drift on down deeper and deeper into relaxation, so calm, so comfortable, so very, very peaceful, I'm going to present some suggestions to your subconscious mind, suggestions which you are going to find reasonable, acceptable, and in your best interests. You are resolving now to forgive yourself for your past sins of procrastination. You are giving up now the self-punishing guilt in favor of honest regret, and you're getting on with the present. You no longer work yourself up into a depression over past things left undone. If you haven't done something, you are not by definition a failure. You are just a person with many, many positive characteristics who has just not done something. If you really can't or don't want to do something, you are being honest with yourself now and with other people involved, so that they can act without you. And if you have to put something off for external reasons, you now request a specific time extension. And if this inconveniences someone, you offer to compensate that person in some other way. But you are resolved to be open about your need to delay your firm resolve to finish. You are learning now to set priorities, recognizing what you have to do; what tasks are most important; if your life is disorganized, you now create a realistic routine that will make it easier for you to keep track of your responsibilities, resolving now to access your needs realistically and honestly. You are identifying what you are willing to do with the present to gain something you want in the future. You now gauge your frustration tolerance. Future rewards are sufficient to keep you working instead of procrastinating. You are now setting practical goals for yourself, breaking down large tasks into more manageable, smaller ones. You learn from your successes, and with these successes you can control your behavior. You practice making rapid decisions on minor issues that have minor consequences . . . For instance, you wear the first appropriate outfit you think of to work or to a party. You order the first appealing item on the lunch menu. You decide whether you want pepper on your salad without taking a poll of the others at your table. You do small tasks that pop into your head immediately if you are not occupied. If you are busy, you make a note and you do the little tasks as soon as you are free, learning now to trust your ability to make decisions. You are focusing now on short time intervals and you are deciding what you are going to do with them . . . Right now, as you sit in that chair, I'd like you to make a clear decision as to what you are going to do in the fifteen minutes after you finish listening to me. And picture and imagine yourself completing this task with abundant and abounding enthusiasm, feeling so good about being able to complete this task. And already you begin to feel the energizing effects of pleasing yourself by fulfilling your responsibilities, feeling now a sense of accomplishment, a sense of well-being, of pride in yourself. Resolving now to keep track of your behavior, realizing now what you like to do and what you don't like to do . . . When you complete a task that you've been avoiding, you reward yourself by doing something that you like to do, perhaps reading, working on a hobby, going to the movies. When you don't complete something, you impose a penalty, a penalty, not a punishment. You might require yourself to do something you dislike, like cleaning up the garage, or getting up early to make lunch for everyone before they leave for work or school. You might also leave motivating notes for yourself, where you can't fail to see them, like on the bathroom mirror, or on the refrigerator, or on the center of your car steering wheel. You are learning now to get in touch with your feelings about doing an uncompleted task, asking yourself how good it would actually feel to get it over with; how much self-criticism is it worth to keep putting it off; what does the task involve, and the risk involved in tackling that particular task ... You practice accepting a certain amount of anxiety and suspense as you take risky actions, thinking of yourself now as a heroic person embarking on a voyage of discovery, even if it is just to get the tires rotated. Resolving now to let go of any performance anxiety you might have, realizing now that doing is the important thing. Doing well is fine, but doing poorly is a frequent and potentially invaluable human experience. It doesn't evaluate you in any manner whatsoever. Resolving now to do better for yourself, telling that part of you to treat you better, to stop sabotaging you — that part of you that procrastinates. You do have control over most of what you do and what you don't do. There is always a choice, and you are making a choice right now to be a person of action, a person who gets things done. And all of these suggestions are implanted deeply, firmly and permanently in the deepest reaches of your subconscious mind, to help you become the person you want to be, will be and deserve to be.

Now in a moment I'm going to awaken you by counting from 1 up to 5. When I reach the count of 5, your eyes will open, and you will be wide awake, completely out of the hypnotic state, awakening with a marvelous feeling of well-being, feeling fine and wonderful in very conceivable way.

Counting now, one, you are beginning to awaken; two, you are completely and totally relaxed; three, you are physically refreshed and mentally alert; and four, you are exceptionally clear-headed; and five, eyes open, wide awake, feeling fine and wonderful."

HYPNOTHERAPY SCRIPT TO ELIMINATE ANGER

". . . And as you continue to drift on down deeper and deeper into relaxation, so calm, so comfortable, so very, very peaceful, I'm going to present some suggestions to your subconscious mind. Suggestions which you will find acceptable, reasonable, and in your best interest.

You are realizing now that anger is the most destructive of all of our emotions because it lies hidden, unrecognized and causes maladjustment. In guilt, we are angry at ourselves; in hate, we are angry at the object of our hatred; in self-pity, we are angry at the situations or people who frustrate us. Anger may be overt, but often it is insidious in its many disguises. Expressed or suppressed, it accounts for most of our misery. No one can become so emotionally mature that they can completely free themselves of anger. But by minimizing it we can lead much, much happier lives. When we succeed in shaking off the chains of hostility, our anger is replaced with pity and possibly even amusement at the emotional naivetë of those who take hostile thrusts at us.

Anger can cause a great amount of unhappiness and it can cause many forms of illness. And it's usually unjustified. When you are angry, your brain is inhibited and therefore you are reduced to something less that your whole human potential. By following these suggestions you will be impressing the desirability of tolerance and understanding upon your subconscious and conscious mind. You'll find yourself at peace with the world and at peace with yourself, because you want to live happily and harmoniously with other people and enjoy good health, physically and emotionally. You now find that you have a feeling of peace and tolerance toward everyone. You like people, people like you. You realize that each personality is a product of heredity and experience. You know that if you had been born with someone else's body and had gone through the exact same experiences in the exact same order as they, you'd probably act exactly as they do. Therefore, you accept others as they are. And when they do things that you disapprove of the only emotions you feel are sympathy, understanding. You are in complete control of your emotions at all times, even under what others believe to be stressful and trying conditions, and this gives you a feeling of great satisfaction. You feel and express only the good healthful emotions of love, sympathy and tolerance toward others. You love other people for their good qualities and you forgive them for the acts that you disapprove of. Because you know that they're doing what anyone else would do with their same body, experience, and levels of awareness. You're a friendly and loving person. You have a kind word and a warm smile for everyone. For this reason you are well-liked. You accept others as they are. And you know that your present disposition often starts a chain reaction, a pleasant feeling in others, and they treat others better as a result, and this makes you feel very, very good. Others like and admire you for your understanding and forgiving nature. You are happy because you know the key to happiness is love and understanding, tolerance and sympathy. You harbor these beneficial emotions, and reject all others. You are a better, more admirable person for your ability to smile at those who are angry. And you find it easy to think clearly and choose the proper words because you are serene and relaxed. You sympathize with others for their bad qualities, and you love them for their good qualities. You are in complete control of your emotions, and only the good and healthy ones are present in your mind. And these healthy emotions feed back into your daily living, and they keep you happy and contented. You enjoy being tolerant, understanding and forgiving. You now forgive everyone for anything they have done. You like people, And you like yourself, you're a tolerant, good person, sympathetic and understanding. You're relaxed and comfortable around other people because of your loving attitude. You like people and you understand people. Your subconscious mind absorbs all of these ideas and feeds them back into your daily living. Your subconscious mind is where the emotions reside. It guides you in selecting good, healthful responses. You are a friendly, warm, loving person. You accept others as they are, and you're in complete control of your emotions at all times. You radiate the good, healthful emotions and reject all others. And you are experiencing personal growth with each and every passing day."

HYPNOTHERAPY SCRIPT TO ELIMINATE GUILT

"... And as you continue to drift on down, deeper and deeper into relaxation, so calm, so peaceful, I'm going to present some suggestions to your subconscious mind, suggestions which you are going to find reasonable, acceptable, and in your best interests. As you drift on down deeper and deeper, you are realizing now that guilt is a form of self-abasement. We punish ourselves by disrupting the vital life functions of the body inviting illness and depression every time you dwell on guilt.

Harboring guilt serves no good purpose. It doesn't right wrongs, and it doesn't help anyone or anything. If you're using guilt as self-punishment you are actually breaking the laws of nature. Everyone makes mistakes, and you have a right to be wrong, but you don't have a right to punish a healthy body and make it sick, even if it does belong to you. And to help rid yourself of guilt you find yourself following certain guidelines. You try to make amends for genuine wrongs, and then get on with living. If you've really caused some harm, you're asking yourself what you can do to make things better. You no longer create a problem where there is none. You also resolve to examine the standards by which you judge yourself. Are they standards you accept? Or have they been imposed upon you by parents, teachers, or employers? You ask yourself if they are reasonable and necessary standards for the way you want to live, or are there other standards which are more meaningful and valid to you. You also resolve to accept your imperfections. Perfection may be a noble and sincere spiritual goal, but it is not part of the condition of human life. Perfection is an unattainable ideal, and it is not a requirement for worthwhile, joyful living. People often have to act without full knowledge of the consequences. For example, even if they try their best, parents can never know enough to deal correctly with all the problems of child rearing. So you no longer burden yourself with unrealistic demands. You no longer expect to be free of anger and oppressive situations. You no longer punish yourself for lack of sexual purity in thought and deed. You are also more and more each day resisting the guilt maneuvers of people like spouses, friends, employers. You are continually on the lookout for the ways other people have made you feel guilty. It's impossible to win universal approval. No matter how hard you try to mold yourself to external demands you're not going to please everyone. And you realize this. The others in your life, however important to you, are all individuals responsible for their own feelings. If you contract on living well and decently in the present, according to standards that count for you, you will be able to deal creatively with other people's criticism or disappointment. You are also making it a point to review yourself, asking yourself what you've actually done that makes you feel guilty, and what you can learn from it. You know that you cannot change the past, but you can learn from it, and you can use this lesson to create a satisfying present. You also remind yourself regularly that past a certain point, you are doing no one a favor by feeling guilty. There is no value to constant, excessive guilt. It's far better to be cheerful and constructive. You now forget your own past bad deeds and those of others. Because you want to have a healthy mind and a healthy body, you hereby forgive yourself for all things you've done in the past. You throw a heavy yoke off your shoulders as you forgive yourself. You forgive yourself and everyone else because you know that we are all products of our heritage and our environment. You want the best for everyone as well as for yourself. You are a loving person, and you live a happy contented life. You have a great feeling of peace and tranquility as you forgive yourself. You start with a clean slate each and every day. During the day as you go about your daily routine, you feel a wonderful new sense of freedom. Perhaps now and then a little thrill runs up your spine as you suddenly remember that you have good feelings toward everyone. You like yourself. And people sense your self-respect and they like you the better for it. You radiate love, kindness and forgiveness for everyone, and for yourself. You are a good, loving person and you deserve happiness and respect. You forgive everyone, and you forgive yourself because forgiveness is good, and you realize this. You feel a great sense of freedom as you forgive yourself, and you find yourself at peace with the world. But especially you are at peace with yourself. You are now turning experiences of guilt into opportunities to clarify what your values really and truly are, and you are practicing the art of self-forgiveness. And you are dedicating yourself each and every day to fully living what you define as a good life in the present. All of these suggestions are now implanted deeply, firmly, and permanently in your subconscious mind to help you eliminate and overcome excessive guilt.

HYPNOTHERAPY SCRIPT FOR FEAR OF CROWDS

You are understanding now that no outside force is making you fear crowds. Your body is simply responding to the way you are thinking. You are learning now to cope with your nervous symptoms as well as with the situations you fear, remembering that panic is a state of physical shock. Blood vessels may dilate or constrict drastically, your brain may be deprived of blood, and faintness may result, but you realize that your body is functioning normally in the circumstances of fear and tension that you are creating for it. Nervous symptoms will cease to come only when their coming no longer matters to you.

So you find yourself now replacing any feelings of fear and panic you feel in crowds with emotions of peace, comfort and tranquility. And to help you to conquer this, I am now going to teach you a very simple, but powerful technique.

Whenever you find yourself in a crowd, I would like you to close your eyes, just for a moment, and take a deep breath. And as you exhale, just picture yourself as calm, peaceful and deeply relaxed as you are now. To reinforce this relaxation, you say or think to yourself five times the word "relax." Then you take another deep breath, exhale, open your eyes and go about your business. And as you do this you immediately begin to relax. All stress, tension and anxiety just fades away, and you find yourself feeling calm, comfortable and relaxed. Now I'd like you to picture and imagine yourself in the middle of a cobblestone village square which is filled with tables and carts.

Now, these carts are laden with all sorts of fruits, vegetables, meats and fish. And the square is thronged with people. But in the midst of this crowd you feel perfectly calm, comfortable and relaxed. You can hear the cries of the vendors as they hawk their wares, hear the voices of the shoppers as they gaily chatter away. And off in the distance you hear the soft chimes of a clock. It chimes once, twice, a third time, a fourth time, now a fifth time. It's five o'clock in the afternoon and as you walk among the carts, the tables and among the crowd you are feeling calm, comfortable and relaxed. You feel the sun warm upon you. But you are not uncomfortable, because a delightful breeze fills the square, having traveled down from tall mountains far off in the distance. Look out at the mountains ... looming tall and dark against an azure blue sky. Feel the cobblestones beneath your feet, the cobblestones worn smooth from centuries of use.

And from a cart off to your left, the delicious aroma of fresh brewed coffee greets your nostrils. And as you walk on, off to your right, the smoky smell of meat being barbecued on wooden skewers over searing, white hot coals, tempts you. But you decide that you're not hungry just yet and you pass on. Now the sun begins to set, going down behind the mountains. Its rays fill the sky with gold, purple, crimson and scarlet hues. And you continue to walk among the tables and the carts, sometimes stopping to sample the wares now.

It's growing darker and darker, and soon the square is lit by lanterns hanging suspended from ropes and wires. And overhead a huge golden moon fills the sky. It arises from behind the mountains where only a short time before the sun went down. The night is warm and comfortable as you walk on, feeling so relaxed. You are guided by the shimmering light from the lanterns, now rustling ever so slightly in the breeze. You are aware of the cries of the vendors, the voices of the crowds, all of the delicious, tempting aromas that fill the night air.

You are enjoying yourself so very, very much. And as you walk on you come upon a cart that is laden with ripe oranges. The scent of oranges is very strong. Smell the oranges. You decide you like the oranges, so you pick one out and you pay the vendor. You stick your fingernail into the rough rind to pierce it so that you may peel the orange. And as you do, the juice spurts out, spraying your hand—you can feel it. You peel the orange and then bite into it. The sweet orange squirts into your mouth and it runs down your throat. Taste the orange.

Continue to walk on, among the crowd, still remaining calm and comfortable, so relaxed. But you are beginning to feel tired. And off to the side of the square you see a bench. You make your way through the crowd and you reach the bench and you sit down, and you can feel the hard boards of the bench beneath you. It feels so good to just rest and relax, and you close your eyes and just let yourself drift.

The sounds and the smells of the square and the crowd fill you with peace and contentment. Now the scene begins to fade, and still deep in the hypnotic state you return to this time and this place and that chair, deep asleep and drifting even deeper. And each and every day, in every conceivable way, you find yourself feeling more calm, comfortable, relaxed, peaceful, serene, tranquil, whenever you find yourself in a crowd, overcoming each and every day any anxiety or tension you ever felt among a crowd. Replacing those feelings with feelings of peace, joy and enjoyment, confident relaxation.

HYPNOTHERAPY SCRIPT FOR IMPROVING YOUR TENNIS

. . . And as you continue to drift on deeper and deeper into relaxation, so calm, comfortable, and very, very relaxed, I'm going to present some suggestions to your subconscious mind. Suggestions which you are going to find reasonable, acceptable and in your best interest, to help you become the tennis player you want to be, will be, deserve to be.

I'd like you to picture and imagine yourself now out on the tennis court. See yourself now watching that tennis ball approaching you. As it crosses the net I want you to see yourself bring your racquet back. Its head is dropping just below your waist, you can see your foot stepping over, pointed at the appropriate side of the court. And you can feel the weight of your body shifting as you make contact with the outside undersurface of the ball. Your stroke moves smoothly forward. See your racquet meeting the ball out in front of you. And you can see yourself watching the ball intently, you can see it sink into the taut racquet strings and compress then travel back toward the top of the net as you complete the stroke. And you feel the head of the racquet move around your body and stop at your side. When the racquet contacts the ball, you visualize the muscles of your forearm, the muscles of your wrist and fingers hold the racquet very firmly and perpendicular to the court surface. You see the ball traveling to a precise spot you have chosen on your opponent's side. And you feel a tremendous wave of excitement and joy at this remarkable accuracy. The ball is returned repeatedly by your opponent to your side and you see yourself returning the ball perfectly each and every time, and it travels to the exact spot you select, without exception. Each time you hit the ball you see in detail each and every move that you make and the moves flow together to create a vivid picture of your perfect stroke.

I'd like you now to picture and imagine a professional tennis player that you've seen play. You've seen this player hitting a perfect stroke and you imagine now that you are that player and you are competing in a major tournament. And you picture the last crucial point of the match as a shot that you hit perfectly, and you can hear the crowd applaud, cheer wildly and you enjoy the praise and admiration given to you. Now see yourself hitting that same perfect shot a hundred times in the next few moments. You observe and you sense every fine detail of the shot. You hear the gratifying sound of the tennis ball meeting the head of the racquet in the exact center; you feel your feet move on the court with exact precision covering the court easily, naturally, gracefully, thus enabling you to meet the ball at the precise moment it should be hit. You hear the whiz of the ball and you can feel the motion of the air around you as you complete your perfect swing. You feel yourself becoming exhilarated as you hit shot after shot with your flawless stroke, finding now and in the future that each and every time you play tennis you are physically free, your body is able to move naturally, seemingly on its own, free of tensions. You may at times even be surprised at your own strength, speed and agility even though there is no strain. You are finding that you are mentally focused, your attention is directed to the action, to the here and now. You find yourself concerned only with making the play and not thinking of the past or the future, finding also that you are in harmony, no part of you conflicts with another. Mind and body work together and you're moving with the action and you have the feeling of being one with that action, also finding that you are enjoying it; the experience is pleasurable—not just in terms of the satisfaction with the results, it simply feels right, finding now that the better you concentrate the better you play. You become more alert to what is happening around you because your attention is now undivided and because you are mentally there for more time than if your mind were wandering. Time indeed seems to slow down for you. You literally feel that you have more time to perform the necessary motions because you are with the activity all of the time, becoming so good at concentration that you seem to be able to tell where the ball is going to be before it gets there with a degree of certainty that you never had before.

To help you attain this perfect concentration, I'm now going to teach you a very simple but very powerful technique. In the future, before a match or at times during the match when you do have the time, I'd like you to take a few moments, go off by yourself, close your eyes and take a deep breath and as you exhale you picture yourself just as calm, peaceful as you are now. Just let your mind drift back to this time and this place ... in that chair so relaxed. And to attain that perfect concentration you say or think to yourself five times the word "concentrate." You then take another deep breath, exhale, open you eyes and go about your business. As you do this you do begin to concentrate. Your thoughts begin to narrow down to the match at hand. You find yourself concentrating totally, vividly on the ball and on the play. All other things seem to just fade away. For you, there exists only the match and you who are playing it. As you move easily, naturally, gracefully making all the moves, all the shots, all the plays.

Now in a moment I'm going to awaken you by counting from 1 up to 5 and when I reach the count of 5 your eyes will open and you'll be wide awake, completely out of the hypnotic state, awakening with a marvelous feeling of well-being, feeling fine, feeling wonderful in every conceivable way.

Counting now, 1—you're beginning to awaken; 2—you're completely and totally relaxed; 3—you're physically refreshed and mentally alert; 4—you are exceptionally clear-headed; and 5-eyes open, wide awake, feeling fine and wonderful.

GLOSSARY

Age Progression	The advancing of a subject's age level while he is in the hypnotic state.
Age Regression	Taking a subject back to "visit" or re-experience earlier times while in the hypnotic state.
Amnesia	The loss of ability to recall past experiences. This sometimes occurs in deep hypnosis, and may be either spontaneous or induced by suggestion.
Anaesthesia or Analgesia	Insensibility to feelings or pain.
Animal Magnetism	As defined by Friedrick Mesmer, a liquid in the body that responds to magnets, and when unequally distributed, causes illness.
Autogenic Training	A term devised by J.H. Schultz of Germany. It consists of a series of mental exercises to produce relaxation: probably related to autohypnosis.

Autohypnosis	Self-hypnosis. Sometimes refers to automatic or spontaneous hypnosis.
Autonomic Nervous System	A part of the peripheral nervous system regulating involuntary responses, especially those concerned with nutritive, vascular and reproductive activities. Recent studies have found, however, that term is a misnomer, as it is possible to control many of the systems once thought to be involuntary.
Autosuggestion	Suggestions one gives oneself, rather than those coming from someone else.
Automatic Writing or Drawing	The hand moves autonomously without the conscious guidance of the subject.
Baquet	French word for tub: a device used by Mesmer in the induction of convulsions.
Belief	A thought pattern, conscious or unconscious, about an event or series of events in an individual's world. A perceived fact or truth.
Belief System	An individual's blueprint of what they experience in life. It is one aspect of the foundation of the human personality complex.

Catalepsy	A condition of suspended animation and loss of voluntary motion in which the limbs hold any position in which they are placed.
Conditioning	A series of inductions making certain ideas or things acceptable to the subject's subconscious mind.
Conscious Mind	The physiological awareness which we consider to be mentality. It is the part which focuses on the physical world.
Davis-Husband Scale	One chart or method of determining depth of hypnosis.
Defense Mechanism	A generally unconscious psychological behavior or belief used to protect oneself from a painful reality.
Direct Suggestion	An idea presented directly to the patient with the hope that he will accept it uncritically and wholeheartedly. Most of the authoritative in the induction techniques are direct suggestions.
Dissociation	The removal of the self from a previous perspective of something in order to view the self from outside that perspective, while still maintaining a model of the same perspective.

Distortion	The process of misrepresenting data in order to change the way the data is internally experienced.
Double-bind	Subject is given a choice of alternatives, either of which leads to the desired result. This has the aspect of permissiveness and the subject finds it difficult to avoid making a choice, but the choice commits him to a course of action. Simple example: Speaking to a young child—"Would you rather go to bed now or in ten minutes?"
Eidetic Imagery	Sensory imagery, primarily visual, which practically reaches the clarity of actual perception. Common in children, rare in adults, but can be readily aroused in hypnosis.
Finger Levitation	The lifting of a finger in an involuntary manner; *i.e.* the subject knows that the finger is lifting but he does not feel that he is lifting it. (See Dissociation).
Flaccidity	Looseness; an absence of muscle tone as seen in persons relaxed in hypnosis
Focal Point or Fascination Point	The object upon which the subject fixes his/her gaze in some hypnotic inductions.

Focus	The fixing of attention to a particular idea which limits the awareness of all other ideas at a given time.
Fractionation	The process of hypnotizing the subject, waking and rehypnotizing a number of times in the same session; an effective means of increasing trance depth.
Free Association	Spontaneous unrestricted associations of loosely linked ideas or images.
Glove Anesthesia	A loss of tactile sensation in the hand, from the wrist to the fingertips.
Group Hypnosis	The use of an induction technique with a group instead of a single individual. For some purposes this is extremely effective.
Hand Levitation	The lifting of the hand in an involuntary manner.
Heterohypnosis	A state of hypnosis into which the subject is helped by another person (contrast with Autohypnosis).
Hypnoanalysis	Psychoanalysis carried on with the aid of hypnosis. The subject shows less inhibition under hypnosis, thus hastening the psychoanalytical process.

Hypnoanesthesia	The blocking of sensation by suggestion (Negative Hallucination). Usually the term refers to the blocking of pain and should properly be termed hypnoanalgesia.
Hypnodisc	A disc with spirals, that is sometimes used, spinning, to help induce hypnosis.
Hypnodontics	The science of dental hypnosis.
Hypnography	A technique whereby the hypnotized subject is brought to express psychological conflicts in drawing or painting.
Hypnodial State	A state resembling sleep in appearance, but more resembling the awake state in body functioning measurements.
Hypnosis	Taken from the Greek word, *hypnos*, meaning sleep; name given to the "sleep-like" trance state by Dr. James Braid, who later regretted it and wanted to change it to a more accurate word, but the original "stuck."
Hypnotic Passes	Those gestures or movements made by the hypnotist over the body of the subject without actually touching the person.

Hypnotherapy	The treatment of disease by using hypnosis; psychotherapy or counseling that facilitates suggestion, reeducation or analysis by means of hypnosis.
Hypnotic Suggestion	A suggestion given while subject is in the hypnotic state and to be carried out while still in hypnosis.
Hysteria	Emotional excitability due to mental cause.
Ideomotor Activity	Involuntary movement produced as the direct expression of an idea rather than reflex. Can be used as a way of signaling or answering the hypnotherapist while in trance.
Imagination	The space-time dimension in which we internally create and experience all thought.
Indirect Suggestion	An idea presented in such a way that the subject does not realize that it is addressed to him. Such a suggestion is likely to bring out less resistance.
Induction Techniques	Methods used to help a subject attain the hypnotic state or trance.

Interpersonal Relationship	The relationship of one person to another. May be of many varieties, as friendly, antagonistic, warm, cold, etc. In connection with clinical hypnosis, the doctor-patient relationship is emphasized. This should be one of confidence, trust and cooperation on the part of the subject, and a sympathetic, permissive attitude on the part of the therapist. It is the therapist's responsibility to establish the proper relationship.
Lethargy	A condition of drowsiness or stupor. Lethargic sleep sometimes used to refer to a light trance state, characterized by little or no post-hypnotic control.
Levels of Hypnosis	Different depths of hypnosis are recognized which determine the type of suggestion the subject will readily accept.
Levitation	The involuntary raising of a part of the body as a result of suggestion. Usually the term is used with reference to a finger, hand or arm.
Mass Hypnosis	Hypnotic induction of a group of people simultaneously.

Mesmerism	Those hypnotic principles advocated by Mesmer.
Mirroring	Temporarily adopting another's behavior in order to achieve rapport with that person.
Monoideism	A term employed by Braid for waking hypnosis and the lighter states of hypnotic sleep.
Narcohypnosis	Light sleep or deep trance state induced by narcotics (such as sodium amytal or pentothal), aided by hypnotic suggestions.
NLP	Neurolinguistic Programming. Neuro refers to the brain and nervous system and linguistic refers to language as it relates to the mind-experience. NLP is a relatively new scientific method of using the way we express our experiences to enhance communication and facilitate change.
Occult	The unseen, or secret; beyond the bounds of ordinary knowledge.
Phobia	An exaggerated and illogical fear of something specific.
Plenary Trance	A state of complete immobility. Subject appears to be in a coma but is not. This condition is rarely seen.

Positive Hallucination	By suggestion, the subject has a sensory experience of something which does not exist.
Positive Suggestion	A suggestion stated in a positive manner; e.g. "Please sit down", versus "Please do not stand."
Posthypnotic Suggestion	Suggestions made during the hypnotic trance to be carried out after awakening.
Prehypnotic Tests	Tests based on reflexes accompanied by suggestion to create certain effects.
Psychosis	A category of mental illnesses, in which there is a loss or distortion of the sense of reality, usually accompanied by delusions or hallucinations.
Psychosomatic	Pertaining to bodily changes stimulated or depressed through mental influence.
Rapport	The process of offering back another's behavior in such a way that trust is created. It is done with matching and mirroring behavior, as well as by empathy and understanding.

Revivification	The patient relives, with a feeling of present reality, a previous experience. These experiences usually have a strong emotional component.
Self-Hypnosis	Placing oneself into a hypnotic state.
Sleep	This term is often used in induction techniques, as "go deeper asleep". It is a misnomer because hypnosis is not sleep.
Somnambulism	The generally recognized greatest depth of hypnosis.
Subconscious Mind	The portion of consciousness that is not in current mental awareness.
Stage Hypnotism	The use of hypnotic techniques for the purpose of entertainment.
Suggestion	An idea that is offered to the subject, usually in hypnosis, to influence behavior and/or thinking. While in hypnosis, suggestions are accepted uncritically.
Tests of Suggestibility	Methods designed to measure the degree of suggestibility of a subject.
Therapeutic	Of or pertaining to the healing arts; curative.

Time Distortion	Unexplained lapse of time or incorrect time perception following hypnosis; sometimes deliberately used in therapy.
Trance	A term used to describe the hypnotic experience. The word "state" may be preferred.
Trance Depth	A measurement of the level or intensity of trance.
Waking Hypnosis	Hypnotic suggestions accepted by the subject in the waking state.

BIBLIOGRAPHY

Ansari, Masud, *Modern Hypnosis.* Mas-press: Washington D.C., 1982.

Copelan, Rachel, *How to Hypnotize Yourself and Others.* Harper & Rowe: New York, 1981.

Coué, Emile, *How to Practice Suggestion and Auto-Suggestion.* American Library Service: New York, 1923.

Davis. L.W. and Husband, R.W., *"Hypnotic Suggestibility in Relation to Personality Traits".* Journal of Abnormal and Social Psychology, 26:175, 1931.

Erickson, Milton H. (Jay Haley, ed.), *Advanced Techniques of Hypnosis and Therapy.* Grune & Stratton, Inc.: New York and London, 1967.

Estabrooks, George H. *Hypnotism.* E.P. Dutton & Co.: New York, 1957.

Gindes, Bernard, *New Concepts of Hypnosis.* Wilshire Book Company: Hollywood, 1951.

Hoorwitz, Aaron Noah, *Hypnotic Methods in Non-Hypnotic Therapies.* Irvington Publishers, Inc.: New York, 1989.

Hull, Clark L., *Hypnosis and Suggestibility.* Appleton-Century: New York, 1933.

Kroger, William S., *Clinical and Experimental Hypnosis.* J.B. Lippincott Co., Philadelphia, 1977.

Le Cron, Leslie and Bordeaux, Jean, *Hypnotism Today.* Grune and Stratton, Inc.: New York, 1947.

Maltz, Maxwell, *Psycho-Cybernetics.* Prentice-Hall, Inc.: Englewood Cliffs, N.J., 1966.

Marcuse, F.L., *Hypnosis-Fact and Fiction.* Penguin Books: Baltimore, 1959.

Restak, Richard, *The Brain.* Bantam Books: New York, 1984.

Schwartz, Herman S., *The Art of Relaxation.* Sessions Publishers: Elmhurst, New York, 1959.

Spiegel, Herbert and Spiegel, David, *Trance and Treatment: Clinical Uses of Hypnosis.* Basic Books, Inc.: New York, 1978.

Weitzenhoffer, Andre' M., and Ernest R. Hilgard. *Stanford Hypnotic Susceptibility Scale.* Consulting Psychologists Press, Inc.: Palo Alto, California, 1959.

Wolberg, Lewis R., *HYPNOSIS: Is it for You?*, Harcourt Brace Jovanovich, Inc.: New York, 1972.

INDEX